MONETARY EQUILIBRIUM
AND ECONOMIC DEVELOPMENT

MONETARY EQUILIBRIUM
AND ECONOMIC DEVELOPMENT

WITH SPECIAL REFERENCE
TO THE EXPERIENCE OF GREECE, 1950—1963

BY XENOPHON ZOLOTAS

PRINCETON UNIVERSITY PRESS

PRINCETON NEW JERSEY

1965

Printed in Athens, Greece
at the Bank of Greece Printing Works

PREFACE

The present study is an attempt to synthesize general economic principles with the practical experience of applying these principles to the "real world" of a developing economy. Thus, the contents of the study are neither purely theoretical nor strictly empirical. The aim has been to obtain an organic sequence in the analysis of concrete problems and situations in a developing country, as influenced by policy measures deriving from general economic principles. The author, an academic economist and, for the last ten years, Governor of the Bank of Greece has undertaken the task in the hope that sharing his experience may be of interest to his colleagues in both the academic and banking world. The book contains at the same time an over-all account of the policies of the Bank of Greece and offers an appraisal of its contribution to the monetary equilibrium and development of the Greek economy.

The main task of the study is to examine from a long-term point of view the problems involved in securing orderly monetary conditions with accelerated economic development. The conclusion is that the maintenance of relative price stability and equilibrium in the balance of payments is not only compatible with a rapid and sustained development process but is, in fact, an indispensable prerequisite of it. At the same time, satisfactory progress towards fulfilling the legitimate aspirations of the people for higher living standards is equally essential to the preservation of monetary equilibrium. In broader perspective, economic development and monetary equilibrium are very closely interrelated and an attempt to treat them as competing policy objectives is inevitably misleading.

The argument is not confined in scope to any particular country, but refers to a range of problems which are generally and mainly applicable to post take-off developing countries. Greek economic experience over approximately the last fifteen years provides the material for an empirical verification of the hypotheses advanced in this study.

I am greatly indebted to the Staff of the Economic Research Department of the Bank of Greece for their valuable assistance in the preparation of this book.

I wish also to express my warm thanks to Professors H.S. Ellis and G. Haberler, who were visiting Greece at the time of the completion of this study, for their most helpful comments and suggestions.

XENOPHON ZOLOTAS

Athens
August 1964

CONTENTS

TABLES

TABLES

x

TABLES

DIAGRAMS

INTRODUCTION

Economic Development Versus Monetary Stability : A Longer-Run View of the Problem

In recent years we have witnessed a mounting controversy on the subject of economic development and monetary stability as competing policy objectives. As the theoretical arguments involved are of direct relevance for developing countries in formulating and implementing their economic policies, an attempt to settle the issue would be of major significance. In spite of the fact, however, that each of the two opposing schools of thought—sometimes designated the "structuralists" and the "monetarists" — encompasses a wide range of views, it seems that somehow the element of time has not received sufficient attention. Yet, proper consideration of the time factor would probably have shown the barrenness of the controversy from a longer-run point of view.

The problem of economic growth and monetary stability offers another example of the difference between the long-run point of view and the short. Experience has shown that for a certain limited period a country can achieve a substantial rate of growth with or without monetary stability, and vice versa. Thus, even though the available statistical evidence suggests a certain degree of complementarity between rates of growth and stable monetary conditions, it is possible in the short run to distinguish between the two objectives and stress the one at the expense of the other. In the longer run, however, and in the context of free economies and democratic societies, the growth of real income and over-all monetary equilibrium, defined to include both the domestic price level and the external sector, are mutually interdependent and both form an integral part of an adequate, consistently sustained process of development. Viewed from a longer perspective, a substantial rate of growth can hardly be sustained

1

without the parallel maintenance of relative monetary stability. Conversely, it is extremely difficult to preserve long-term monetary equilibrium in an economy that does not grow at a rate adequate to satisfy the legitimate claims of a population with rising expectations and one increasingly exposed to the influence of the "demonstration effect" of the international scene. The longer-term interdependence of economic growth and monetary equilibrium renders futile the effort to regard them as alternatives in the configuration of priorities for policy objectives. As a matter of fact, undue emphasis on either growth rates or the degree of monetary stability would put in jeopardy both objectives instead of promoting the objective which has been given priority.

It should be stressed at the outset that the above remarks, as to the long-term relationship between economic development and monetary equilibrium, are especially applicable to free economies and democratic societies. In such a socio-economic environment the key role of individuals as producers, consumers, savers, and investors imposes as a *conditio sine qua non* for a successful growth process, the establishment and maintenance of confidence. This confidence, however, should relate not only to the prevalence and safeguarding of orderly monetary conditions, but also to the actual possibility of fulfilling the aspirations of the public for higher standards of living and welfare. Experience has shown that a lack of confidence in the soundness of monetary conditions renders the adoption of development-conducive behavioral patterns by the people of low-income countries particularly hard, if not impossible in the long run. Similarly, the maintenance of over-all monetary equilibrium in an inadequately growing economy becomes extremely difficult in the long run owing to the existence of powerful social forces, often in the form of organized groups (trade unions, farmers, etc.), pressing for rising levels of income and employment. Consequently, the developing democratic countries of the world should face economic growth and

2

monetary stability as a single, inseparable issue.

In a centrally planned economy on the other hand, the limited role left to private initiative and choice and the control of social forces by the state permits us to trace a certain dichotomy between economic development and monetary stability. It should be noted, however, that even a centrally planned socioeconomic regime cannot completely ignore the long-term interdependence between economic growth and monetary order without endangering its own stability.

The outcome of this discussion on the interconnection of growth rates and orderly monetary conditions has some interesting long-run implications when the issue is considered on a short-term basis. In the first place, prolonged and pronounced inflationary financing should be excluded as a deliberate instrument of growth. Secondly, the one-sided pursuit of monetary stability can only be justifiable for a limited period of time, particularly when the impact of "runaway" inflation has rendered the stabilization of prices a basic precondition for the beginning or resumption of a successful growth effort. However, before we enter into a discussion of the short-term aspects of the problem it is necessary to define explicitly the terms "adequate rate of development" and "relative monetary stability."

The Notions of "Relative Monetary Stability" and "Adequate Rate of Development"

If a country is to undertake a successful and consistent development effort, the monetary authorities must have a clear understanding of the requirements of monetary equilibrium, including both the domestic price level and the balance of payments. They must also be ready to forestall inflationary pressures, of which the magnitude and source of origin could jeopardize the over-all development process. It is particularly hard to succeed in this task because,

3

while the extensive and rapid mobilization of resources for development purposes requires the creation of an effective expansionary impulse, the point beyond which the concomitant price increases become dangerous depends on psychological factors and foreign price movements. There is, consequently, ample room for doubt as to the optimum timing and size of the required corrective action in each case.

Monetary equilibrium and inflation are relative concepts extending to a wide range of situations, which cannot be divided into stable or inflationary by any rigid dividing line. The concept of monetary stability should hardly be restricted to the limited meaning of constant prices, but should also include those instances in which the rise in the domestic price level does not substantially diverge from the general upward trend of prices in the international economy. Thus, a country in which price movements keep in line with corresponding developments abroad, without causing undue pressure on its external sector, should be considered, in principle, to be in monetary equilibrium. We are fully aware of the fact that our interpretation of the concepts of monetary stability and equilibrium—used interchangeably in this study—refers to the normative connotations usually attached to these terms. In this sense and in view of the growing interdependence of national economies, the evaluation of monetary conditions in terms of intertemporal comparisons of price changes within an economy should always be supplemented by international comparisons of price movements. In a world of fixed exchange rates and rising prices, it is impossible for any one country to maintain absolute monetary stability in terms of both the internal and external value of its currency. We believe that it would be rather unrealistic and fruitless for a developing country to seek to maintain a constant domestic price level and accept an undervaluation of its currency as a result of the upward trend of prices in the world economy.

With respect to inflation, it is basic to realize that its

4

over-all economic and social impact operates mainly through psychological channels and, consequently, subjective elements play a major role in determining its potential threat. In the case of inflationary tendencies, as in many others, the over-all effect of rising prices depends not so much on the actual magnitude of the increase as on its impact on the minds of the public. The same rate of inflation could pass largely unnoticed, and cause no disturbance in an economy characterized by widespread money illusion, while in an inflation-conscious economy it may induce serious reactions and develop into a full-fledged price-wage spiral. The sensitivity of the public in general to price developments is the main factor determining the limit beyond which inflationary pressures become imminently dangerous. Rising prices in relation to world price levels should be checked just before they begin to have an appreciable adverse influence on consumption and saving habits, entrepreneurial attitudes, and the over-all behavior pattern of the economy. Thus, both objective and subjective factors, namely the actual rise in prices and the psychological reaction of the public, should be taken into account in assessing the degree of stability compatible with an effective development process. On the basis of these considerations, whenever we refer to inflation we have in mind a continuous, pronounced increase in domestic prices, substantially in excess of parallel developments abroad and tending to violate the psychological tolerance limit of economic agents.

The people of less-developed countries appear to be highly sensitive to overt inflationary pressures and external deficits. In many of these countries extended periods of rapid and even galloping inflation have subjected the general public to a hard-to-forget learning process. Owing to their past experience, the people of less-developed countries show a high degree of sensitivity, not only with respect to changes in the general price level but also with respect to special increases in basic commodities or items of great psychological import. For this reason, in many low-income countries an accidental rise in the prices of certain key commodities or gold is often enough to set in motion defensive reactions threatening monetary equilibrium more imminently than is the case in mature economies. In consequence, it is the duty of responsible authorities in less-developed economies to safeguard monetary equilibrium by constant surveillance and prompt regulation not only of aggregate magnitudes but also of certain specific prices and expenditures.

In general, the degree to which a developing country can push its development effort without unduly disturbing the internal and external equilibrium depends significantly on its recent monetary experience. There is a marked difference between restoring monetary order in an inflation-ridden economy and maintaining monetary equilibrium as a joint condition for economic development. In the former case, the establishment of financial stability appears as the primary policy goal, the achievement of which determines the ability of the economy to take off on a sustained development course. In the latter case, the responsible authorities have to keep within appropriate limits the inflationary pressures caused by the development process. These limits, however, are determined to a considerable extent by the experience of the past, of which the inflationary overtones are carried over in the form of psychological sensitivity to price movements. Long after orderly monetary conditions have been established, the stability of the state of confidence remains precarious and requires the utmost care in the expansionary financing of the economy. Nevertheless, it is essential that this expansionary financing be effected on a scale adequate to support a satisfactory rate of growth. The establishment and maintenance of confidence in monetary conditions would be temporary and sterile if unaccompanied by confidence in the economic future of the country. On this basis, an adequate rate of growth may be defined as one which satisfies the legitimate aspirations of the population of a low-income country in such a way as to be consistent with the maintenance of monetary and political order. Obviously, the actual magnitude of an adequate growth rate would differ for every country, depending on the prevailing objective and subjective factors and conditions in each case. At the international level, however, it is essential that the less advanced countries of the world should be assisted to reduce the gap which now separates them from the industrial countries.

ECONOMIC DEVELOPMENT AND INFLATION IN THE SHORT RUN

The origins of the inflationist argument, in the context of the theory of economic growth, should be traced to a false parallelism between the policies recommended in advanced economies in a state of depression on one hand, and underdeveloped economies plagued by extensive open and disguised unemployment on the other. The parallelism ends, however, as soon as it becomes evident that in less-developed countries the core of the problem is not the inadequacy of effective demand in relation to potential supply, but the structural defects of the economy as regards the complementarity of factors of production, with entrepreneurial and organizational skills often more scarce than capital. Unemployment margins and limited "pockets" of excess capacity can hardly determine the productive potential of underdeveloped economies, of which the aggregate supply function is hampered by serious bottlenecks and tends to be intersected at its highly inelastic segment by the aggregate demand curve, following a drastic credit-induced expansion of demand. Under these conditions any excessive increase in the supply of money would result in rising prices and external deficits, with real income virtually unchanged or even falling, if the situation is allowed to deteriorate into hyperinflation.

It appears useful to underline again here a point we have repeatedly made in the past—the serious limits imposed

7

on the absorptive capacity of a low-income country by the shortage of skilled labor, the inadequacy of managerial skills and the over-all organizational inefficiency characteristic of both the public and private sectors of the economy. These handicaps to the development process are often more serious than the limited availability of investment funds and reflect the low educational and training standards in less-developed countries. Experience has shown that quite often the demand for capital to finance ventures conducive to economic growth has lagged behind the corresponding supply, indicating a greater scarcity in business initiative than in investment funds. The unfavorable conditions outlined, which by determining the absorptive capacity of the economy constitute the essence of underdevelopment, point to the necessity for a most judicious utilization of deficit-financing methods in less-developed countries. At the same time, it is more than evident that development programs must put more emphasis and a higher degree of priority on the relatively overlooked problem of the wide extension and rapid improvement of technical education in low-income countries.

It has become widely accepted that monetary "magic" is ineffective and detrimental as a weapon against the real obstacles to economic development. A modified version of the inflationist argument was, therefore, in order. It has thus been argued that prices should be allowed to rise in selected economic sectors, while maintaining price stability in the rest of the economy. The change in relative prices would facilitate the reallocation of resources according to desirable priorities through the market mechanism, which is probably a more effective signalling device in view of the administrative weaknesses of the planning system in less-developed countries. Irrespective of the question-mark as to the efficacy of the incentives to be created by "selective inflation," there are serious doubts with respect to the feasibility of an eclectic inflationary policy. The propagation process of inflation could hardly be confined within the desirable sectoral limits

8

through the weapons of fiscal and monetary policy available in less-developed countries. The imposition of direct controls, on the other hand, would defeat the purpose of alleviating the burden on the administrative system and it is very doubtful whether such measures would ultimately succeed in insulating the rest of the economy from the spread of inflation. Lastly, in view of factor immobility in underdeveloped economies, the increase of prices in the leading sectors would have to be very pronounced—consequently, more difficult to control—in order to effect a substantial, if any, mobilization and transfer of resources. Inflationary pressures on key sectors of the economy are a typical characteristic of the development effort, indicating intensive utilization of available resources. To allow, however, such pressures to develop into open, if selective, inflation, appears quite hazardous as a policy line.

The "forced-saving" aspect of the inflationary process usually occupies a prominent place in the inflationist argumentation. The inflation-induced redistribution of income in favor of the entrepreneurial class, it is argued, would free resources devoted previously to the satisfaction of the consumption needs of the rest of the population, while rising profits would provide a powerful stimulus for investment activity of a cumulative character through the ploughing back of such profits.

The implicit assumptions on which the validity of this proposition depends are both numerous and stringent in the context of backward economies. Since the entrepreneurial class is in relatively short supply quantitatively and qualitatively, it is a typical characteristic of economic backwardness that conspicuous consumption and hoarding, rather than productive investment, are more likely to absorb a substantial part of the higher profits of businessmen in underdeveloped economies. Whatever inducement to invest is created under these conditions is likely to channel additional funds to the traditional, inflation-safe activities, notably real estate

9

purchases and gold, which will prove most profitable in the context of rapidly rising prices. It is hardly necessary to emphasize that in underdeveloped countries the problem of the appropriate utilization of available resources is closely connected with the problem of increasing their availability. Furthermore, in view of the low standard of living of the population in such countries, it is rather doubtful whether in most cases inflation could transfer any substantial resources from consumption to investment without affecting the efficiency of the labor force and without initiating a price-wage spiral. In any case, the inflationary financing of the development effort through "forced savings" on the part of the wider masses of the population, and particularly of the lower income groups, would probably suffice as a cause of frustration and resentment to undermine the very development effort it purports to support. A primary condition for a high and sustained rate of economic development is the enthusiastic and effective participation of the entire population in the process. Such participation could hardly be expected from the bulk of the population, since inflation shifts the burdens and sacrifices arbitrarily and inequitably on the people while it improves the relative position of profit receivers, among whom speculators often outnumber entrepreneurs. In the initial stages of economic development welfare considerations may be subordinate to the requirements of rapid growth, but basic disregard of equity, as in the case of the inflationary effects on the relative position of lower income classes, is likely to jeopardize the success of the over-all development policy.

The inflationist argument refers, as a rule, to some form of controlled inflation, while rapid or galloping inflation is hardly ever recommended as a deliberate policy for economic development. It would, therefore, be less than fair to reinforce the argument against the advocates of controlled inflation by pointing to the detrimental effects of rapid inflation. In view, however, of the ease with which controlled inflation may deteriorate into a rapid, continuous rise in prices and external deficits, it may be useful to summarize the well-known consequences of galloping inflation.

The cornerstone of equilibrium in a free enterprise economy is confidence. The shattering of confidence by inflation is reflected throughout the economy. The pattern of production and investment is distorted in favor of the speculative and least productive activities. Consumption demand rises substantially in anticipation of price increases. Whatever saving is effected under "runaway" inflationary conditions usually takes the form of hoarding gold, foreign exchange, and even nonperishable commodities, in view of the continuous fall in the real value of financial assets denominated in domestic currency. In short, the price mechanism becomes an increasingly distorted and quite misleading signalling device for efficient resource allocation. At the same time, the balance of payments position deteriorates continuously. On current account, imports rise to satisfy the excess domestic demand, while exports fall as a result of the increase in their prices and the diversion of resources from the export industries to domestic speculative activities. On capital account, any previous inflow of capital is rapidly reversed into an outflow of funds. Foreign lenders and investors are not usually inclined to risk their capital in an inflation-ridden economy in which spiralling costs absorb profit margins, while the danger of tighter restrictions and controls appears imminent. On the other hand, the fear of devaluation and, possibly, of social and political upheavals induced by the economic and social disintegration usually caused by rapid inflation, initiates a massive flight of capital abroad. Under these conditions the depletion of foreign exchange reserves is only a matter of time. Furthermore, experience has shown that, in an inflationary context, the efficacy of restrictive measures and direct controls is very limited in all directions, except in creating black markets and drastically curtailing consumers' choice.

The incompatibility of economic development and pronounced inflation rests basically on the effects of the latter on behavioral patterns. The primary condition for the development of a free enterprise economy is a drastic change in the attitudes of economic agents: businessmen should be transformed from quick profit seekers and speculators into creative entrepreneurs; savers should relinquish their hoarding habits and make available their savings for productive utilization through the banking system and the capital market; consumers should be induced to increase their savings; investors should become capable of perceiving the profitability of productive ventures and of estimating future prospects in terms of periods longer than a few months or years. The indispensable prerequisite for effecting these changes is the establishment and maintenance of over-all confidence in monetary, economic and political conditions. It is only through strengthening the state of confidence that "economic horizons" can be expanded in less developed countries. A limited "economic horizon" is a basic reason for the persistence in low-income countries of traditional, unproductive activities and a major obstacle to the adoption of development-conducive patterns of behavior. Continuous, spiralling inflation undermines the state of confidence, rewards speculators and gold hoarders and in general fosters a climate of behavioral backwardness. In the last analysis, this is the reason why less developed countries are less able to afford ventures into inflationary financing for their growth effort than those which are economically advanced. At the same time, however, we should not fail to stress the fact that while monetary stability is a necessary condition for development, it is not in addition a sufficient one. As a rule, major structural changes are required to put a backward economy firmly on the path of development. The implementation of structural readjustments in a developing country often creates serious inflationary pressures. We believe, however, that to allow such pressures to develop into overt inflation would hardly contribute to the realization of the structural changes needed.

On the other hand, we should take seriously into account the limits imposed on the authorities of developing countries in pursuing a policy of financial restraint, by the requirements of a minimum adequate rate of growth, as previously defined. Considerations of political and social feasibility often render inoperative suggestions for controlling the expansion of monetary magnitudes. The implied short-term retardation of the development rate is, in several instances, beyond the capability or daring of political authorities, even though in the long run the continuation of inflation is certain to cause a serious setback in the development process. This is liable to be the case when the maintenance of over-all monetary equilibrium becomes incompatible with an adequate rate of growth as a result of unfavorable developments in the export markets of the countries concerned. The problem of instability in the export market of primary-producing countries and the necessity for international corrective action in this respect are too well known to be discussed further here. In consequence, the improvement of the position of developing countries in world trade and the supplementing of their resources with an adequate flow of development capital appears to be an indispensable prerequisite to both a successful growth process and the prevalence of orderly monetary conditions on a worldwide basis.

THE GOALS OF ECONOMIC POLICY IN A DEVELOPING COUNTRY

The basic goal of economic policy is to improve the material welfare of the people without drastically affecting the prevailing pattern of moral and social values. For democratic societies, this constraint has the direct implication that the growth process, necessary to raise over-all economic welfare, must be effected in the institutional context of a free-enterprise economy, in which government initiative and planning leave ample room to private economic activity.

Thus, in the light of its basic goals and the existing institutional constraints, the main objectives of economic policy in free-enterprise economies amount to the consistent pursuit of:

a) the highest rate of growth permitted by existing resources and the pressing immediate needs of the population;

b) the safeguarding of relative price stability within the limits set by psychological factors and price developments abroad; and

c) the maintenance of equilibrium in the balance of payments.

It is of crucial significance that the goals of economic policy should be clearly and concisely formulated to provide the responsible authorities with operational directives for specific action and also to make these objectives widely understood and effectively supported by the public.

The development target of economic policy implies a maximization problem, subject to the constraint of resource availability for development purposes and the constraint of monetary equilibrium. The first constraint, however, being the residual difference between total available resources and the proportion to be absorbed by current private and public consumption, is itself subject to policy manipulations. The magnitude of the resources—notably capital, entrepreneurship, skilled labor and foreign exchange—to be devoted to the development effort depends: (a) on the volume of total available resources, both domestic and external in origin, which are in turn largely determined by the effectiveness of economic policy in mobilizing resources and (b) on the level and rate of increase through time of consumption standards, which again can be substantially influenced by economic policy.

As regards the task of over-all resource mobilization,

14

including foreign capital and entrepreneurship, there is strong evidence that it can best be effected and sustained under conditions of relative price stability and external equilibrium. At the same time, however, the very essence of the development process requires the creation of an effective expansionary impulse, which will secure a high rate of utilization of available resources. This impulse is especially necessary in view of the limited factor mobility and the slow reactions of businessmen in less-developed countries. The responsible authorities should also keep in mind the characteristic sensitivity of underdeveloped economies to the appearance of pronounced inflationary tendencies. There is, therefore, a problem of optimization of the expansionary impulse which can also be stated in terms of the optimum degree of inflationary pressures allowed to develop by the monetary authorities. The precise and general formulation of the conditions for optimization encounters serious difficulties in this particular case, owing to the prominent role of psychological factors and the peculiar characteristics of each economy, not to mention the usual inadequacy of statistical and analytical information on over-all and sectoral capacities and on the prospective structure of demand. The mobilization of over-all resources is, therefore, usually effected in terms of a trial and error process during which the expansionary impulse often violates the escape valves of rising prices and external deficits. Such pressures are unavoidable as a rule, because of the limited ability to estimate the point beyond which the expansionary impulse will cause price increases and external deficits, rather than growth in real income. This is accentuated by the lack of appropriate supply elasticities in the various sectors of the economy. Furthermore, some measure of pressure on the price level and the balance of payments serves as a positive indication that the development effort is not falling short of the respective potential of the economy.

When we turn to the level and rate of increase of

consumption through time in a developing country, the problem always arises of the intertemporal distribution of the necessary sacrifices and the benefits associated with the development process. In a democratic society, the interplay of consumers' preferences and economic policy determine in each period the distribution of total available resources in this respect. This is a matter of value judgment in view of the intertemporal and interpersonal comparisons of utility involved, not to mention the prominent role of political considerations. In a more general normative context, however, we must stress the narrow margin within which it is desirable and feasible to curtail consumption in favor of savings and investment. As a matter of fact, that such a margin exists at all is due mainly to the consumption-reducing/ saving-increasing potential of the small group of high-income receivers and wealth-owners in less-developed countries. The masses of population, close to subsistence levels, should usually be called upon to make their contribution to the development effort in terms of foregone improvements in their living standards, rather than in terms of positive sacrifices. In other words, the increase in the saving of lower income classes should come out of growing income, with consumption rising at a slower than "normal" rate, and not out of a decline in living standards.

Economic policy has at its disposal a wide variety of tools, ranging from moral suasion to increased taxation of income and consumption. Although the more compulsory tools of economic policy also have their value, in this case it is the effectiveness of persuasion in relation to the present requirements and future benefits of economic development that largely determines the success of a growth policy.

The development of a free enterprise economy and a democratic society is basically a voluntary process. The wholehearted participation and support of the entire population is, therefore, indispensable. To this end, economic policy should give people a taste of the development benefits as soon as possible, in terms of rising standards of living. By the same reasoning, it is necessary and desirable that economic policy should contribute towards a more equitable distribution of income without causing, however, a major decline in the over-all saving level. At the same time, those in control of economic policy should undertake an extensive campaign informing the people about the requirements for economic development that lead to higher incomes and consumption standards. This basic economic fact—rapid economic development cannot be sustained if the largest part of income increases is absorbed by current consumption—should be accepted and supported by all responsible political and social leaders, including trade union officials and all those influencing public opinion. The people should realize that a point may be reached where they can raise their current consumption only at the expense of lower standards of living in the future for themselves and their children. A "hand-to-mouth" policy in low-income countries merely leads to a perpetuation of backwardness and should be rejected outright by all responsible members of society, even when it appears in the guise of a suggestion for a rise in the living standard. It should be made generally clear that in a growing economy a sacrifice in terms of foregone improvements in consumption levels will be more than compensated by the resulting increase in income, a few years later. The tendency of the public to discount excessively the value of future improvements in income and consumption should be counteracted by an efficient information policy, carried out on a wide scale. It is very important that as wide a consensus of public opinion as possible should be in agreement with government objectives for present and future levels of living standards. Quite often, if a particular socio-economic group is dissatisfied with its standard of living and makes an effort to increase its share of the national product, this may be enough to start a chain of defensive reactions on the part of other groups, leading to monetary disequilibrium and retardation of the development process. Should this happen, the more compulsory tools of economic policy would have to be used to correct these tendencies.

If we assume that an effective mobilization of over-all resources is under way and that a generally acceptable decision on consumption standards through time has been taken, the residual difference between the two determines the resources available for development purposes. A crucial task of economic policy is to maximize the rate of growth obtainable from the utilization of these resources. The task requires the optimization of the "investment-mix" through the creation of strong incentives for productive ventures, through measures reconciling social productivity with private profitability and, possibly, through the direct participation of the state in economic activity. On the other hand, effective measures should be taken to discourage investment which does not make a significant contribution to economic development. The classical tools of economic policy are often not available or ineffective for this purpose. Modified and even new organizational methods and instruments of economic policy have to be devised to adapt the pattern of capital formation to the established set of priorities and to obtain the most effective channelling of funds and skills into development-conducive activities.

The over-all responsibility of economic policy in developing countries is, however, even more complicated. The logical scheme previously described, according to which the resources available for development purposes are equated with the residual difference between total available resources and consumption requirements, hardly ever finds its exact counterpart in the real world. The rule in this case is to set a development target that is considered satisfactory on the basis of an approximate estimation of over-all resources available and the needs and aspirations of consumers. This rough form of planning, which frequently leads to inconsistencies, is often the only feasible, rapid method of approach—at least in the early stages of development. In such a context, the task of economic policy and particularly of monetary authorities attains the dimensions characteristic of a "disequilibrium economy." This means that the responsible authorities must stand ready to correct at each moment and phase of the development process the disequilibrating tendencies arising from inconsistencies which are the result of imperfect application of the economic calculus. In this connection it is often hard to distinguish between the appearance of inflationary pressures as a result of "overinvestment" and a general effort on the part of the people to improve consumption standards. Obviously the degree to which such pressures should and can be suppressed depends on their origin. "Overinvestment" is capacity creating and in the longer run tends, to a certain degree, to be self-correcting as regards its inflationary impact. An excessively rising consumption demand, on the other hand, does not contribute to the development process. At the same time, it points to the inadequacy of the persuasion effects of economic policy, and its curtailment should be attempted with the utmost care.

The balance of payments of countries in the process of development usually plays the dual role of an escape valve for excessive absorption of goods and services and a generator of expansionary or contractionary impulses. In the first instance, the viewing of balance of payments developments and the evolution of domestic economic magnitudes as an integral process has shown that an external deficit is often the result of the effort of a country to live or grow beyond its means. From this point of view, rising prices and external deficits are manifestations arising from the same basic cause. For this reason the concept of monetary equilibrium should always encompass developments in the price level and in the balance of payments.

In the second instance, changes in receipts from exports and invisibles and capital inflow have often been an autonomous cause of expansion or contraction in external assets, affecting living standards and the rate of growth. Instability in the export markets of primary-producing countries, most of which are in the process of development, offers a typical example. Another example in recent years is the spectacular rise of invisible receipts in the Greek balance of payments. In both instances, economic policy should take a long-term view of developments in the balance of payments before proceeding to the adoption of drastic corrective measures and adapting the pace of the economy to them.

The balance of payments as a limit to the absorption of an economy is of basic significance. Dwindling foreign exchange reserves would mark the violation of the limit. The approach of the point of exhaustion would have to be countered by import restrictions and exchange controls, the relative ineffectiveness and detrimental results of which are well-known and become even more pronounced in the present context of a world moving rapidly towards increased liberalization of trade and payments. The ultimate consequence, but not necessarily the cure, of persistent deficits in the over-all balance of payments caused by over-absorption, would be devaluation. In fact, devaluation is a self-inducing phenomenon, owing to the impact of rumors on import payments and export receipts as well as on flow of capital. Devaluation is most likely to be an ineffective remedy, if it is not supplemented by the appropriate monetary and fiscal policies that would have rendered it unnecessary if adopted in the first place.

The establishment and maintenance of longer-term equilibrium in the balance of payments is a basic condition for monetary order and a sustained development process. The state of confidence depends significantly on the relative adequacy of foreign exchange reserves and the stability of the exchange rate. Foreign exchange reserves may, of course, be allowed to fluctuate in their role as a "buffer" against seasonal or cyclical fluctuations in receipts and payments, but the stability of the exchange rate must be safeguarded, except in cases where serious maladjustments of a structural character call for the establishment of a more realistic par value.

Mounting pressures on the balance of payments are usually a sign that the economy seeks to operate beyond its means and should always be of concern to responsible authorities. The evaluation, however, of their eventual threat depends on the origin of the deficit-creating forces. It makes quite a difference whether a country tries to live or to grow beyond its means. In other words, external deficits may be the result of either "overconsumption" or "overinvestment" or both. It goes without saying that, in order to determine whether the pressures on the external sector originate from excessive consumption or overinvestment the responsible authorities should look at the global magnitudes in question and not just at the composition of the import list. Rising imports, as a matter of fact, are both a result of and a prerequisite for rising incomes, particularly when the import content of capital formation is high, as is the case with heavy machinery and equipment in most low-income countries. Economic policy should never lose sight of this dual role of imports.

If rising pressures on the balance of payments are caused by overconsumption, the responsible authorities should begin to restrain consumption through fiscal, monetary and commercial policy measures. If, however, overinvestment is the origin of the pressures, the responsible authorities should seek, before applying any drastic measure of retrenchment, to expand total available resources through external financing and through a judicious utilization of foreign exchange reserves—provided that the investment is highly productive and of a relatively short gestation period. An increase in the external indebtedness of the economy and a moderate depletion of foreign exchange reserves can probably be justified if they satisfy a greater investment demand, which conforms to the established set of priorities.

At the same time every effort should be made to improve the export side of the trade balance. Except in the case of a dual economy, where an advanced export-oriented sector has little effect on the over-all rate of progress, an improvement in export capacity and markets should be a major policy goal in developing countries. This is the only way to overcome the obstacles to the adoption of modern technology and organizational methods created by the small size of these countries' markets. Again, in a world of more liberalized trade and payments, rising exports are a positive indication of improved competitiveness, resulting from a more efficient utilization of resources. The development of export-oriented industries on the basis of dynamic considerations is, in fact, a most promising line towards the modernization of organization and technology, and leads to the mutually advantageous integration of the economies of developing countries in the community of advanced nations.

PART ONE

ECONOMIC POLICY IN GREECE SINCE 1950
PROBLEMS AND METHODS

I

A SUMMARY OF DEVELOPMENTS

IN THE GREEK ECONOMY SINCE 1950

INTRODUCTION

The year 1950 marked the end of a turbulent decade for Greece. From 1940 onwards, the country experienced in swift succession, external aggression, enemy occupation, and guerrilla war—all combined to dislocate and bring to a bare minimum the economy's productive capacity. Thus, reconstruction could and did begin only with the end of the guerrilla war in 1950. Since that year, substantial rates of expansion have characterized most sectors of the Greek economy. Significantly, expansion was accompanied by the restoration of internal and external monetary stability and the elimination of restrictions on imports. The rapid expansion in output and income since 1950 has not, however, been associated as yet with a radical change in the structure of the Greek economy.

The main obstacles to a sustained and rapid process of development are the limitations of the human factor in low-income countries, as reflected in the quantitative and qualitative inadequacies of entrepreneurship, the weaknesses of the administrative machine, and the shortage of an experienced labor force. Improvement and extension of the educational standards of the population, with special emphasis on technical and organizational training appears to be the only way to overcome the obstacles to an accelerated rate of growth.

In Greece, education and training have recently been the object of special attention and decisive measures of support. These policies, together with measures facilitating favorable readjustments of the over-all structure of the Greek economy, aim at securing an accelerated rate of economic development.

TABLE 1

Average annual increase in gross national income and per capita income
at 1954 prices between 1950 and 1961. Gross per capita income
in U. S. dollars in selected countries in 1961

Countries	Percentage annual increase in gross national income at 1954 prices	Percentage annual increase in per capita income	Gross per capita income in 1961 at factor cost and in 1954 U. S. dollars
Austria	5.8	5.6	626
Belgium	2.9	2.3	1,122
Canada	3.9a	1.3a	1,598c
Denmark	3.4	2.6	1,030
France	4.4	3.5	1,134
W. Germany	7.5	6.3	943
GREECE	6.5	5.5	322d
Italy	6.3	5.6	547
Netherlands	4.7	3.4	739
Norway	3.8	2.5	994
Portugal	4.5b	4.1b	222c
Sweden	3.6	2.9	1,296
United Kingdom	2.4	2.0	987
U.S.A.	3.4	1.4	2,231

a 1950-1960
b 1952-1960
c 1960
d Net per capita income

Sources: U.N., *Statistical Yearbook* 1961.
O.E.C.D., *General Statistics,* November 1962.
U.N., *Monthly Bulletin of Statistics,* December 1960, October 1962.
I.M.F., *International Financial Statistics,* February 1962.
Ministry of Coordination, *National Accounts of Greece 1948-1959, 1958-1962.*
National Statistical Service of Greece, *Statistical Yearbook 1962.*

NATIONAL INCOME

Between 1950 and 1963, gross national income at 1954 prices rose at an average annual rate of 6.3 per cent, while net per capita income increased by 5.4 per cent, from $178 in 1950 to $353 in 1963. Although these growth rates are higher than those observed in most western countries during the same period, they do not, of course, imply that Greece is no longer a low-income country. This fact becomes quite obvious when the current level of per capita income in Greece is compared with the respective average level in the E.E.C. countries, where it is almost three times higher, or with per capita income in the United States, where it is about seven times higher.

In greater analysis, national income in Greece increased between 1950 and 1957 at an average annual rate of 6.9 per cent. This high rate of income growth should be attributed to the fact that in the early part of the period reconstruction was still under way. Consequently, there were many highly productive opportunities which could be exploited quickly; on the other hand, the income at the base period was very low and high proportional rates of increase in fact reflected less important absolute increases in income.

After 1957, the growth rate of national income slowed down somewhat, in spite of the great improvement in the over-all climate for investment and production. The decline of the average annual rate of growth from 6.9 per cent between 1950 and 1957 to 5.7 per cent in the period 1957 to 1963, reflects chiefly the limited ability of the Greek economy to expand owing to basic structural weaknesses, which it has not yet been possible to eradicate completely. For instance, although the share of primary production in gross domestic product decreased from 34 per cent in 1950 to 31 per cent in 1961 and to 30 per cent in 1963, it is still very high in comparison with corresponding percentages in developed economies.

27

TABLE 2

Composition of gross domestic product in selected countries
(at current factor cost)

Countries	Primary production as percentage of domestic product		Secondary production as percentage of domestic product		Services as percentage of domestic product	
	1950	1961	1950	1961	1950	1961
Austria[a]	16	11[b]	49	51[b]	35	38[b]
Belgium	9	7[b]	46	46[b]	45	47[b]
Denmark	21	14	35	38	44	48
France[c]	15	9	47	44	38	47
W. Germany[c]	11	6	47	57	42	37
GREECE	34	31	25	27	41	42
Italy	29	17	35	42	36	41
Netherlands	14	10	38	42[d]	48	48
Norway	15	12[b]	37	35[b]	48	53[b]
United Kingdom	6	4	46	45	48	51

[a] Gross national product at market prices
[b] 1960
[c] At market prices
[d] Including electric power
   Sources: U. N., *Statistical Yearbooks 1958* and *1962.*
National Accounts of Greece 1948-1959 and *1958-1962.*

In consequence, fluctuations in primary production —
usually caused by crop cycles and weather conditions
—substantially affect the progress of the whole economy. In
effect, the relative slow-down observed in the growth rate of
national income during the second five-year period is largely
attributable to a decline in the rate of increase of agricultural
production.

THE AGRICULTURAL SECTOR

The increase in agricultural output between 1950 and 1963
was achieved by expanding the existing productive capacity,

without any substantial changes in the pattern of agricultural production. In this connection, it is worth noting that the share of animal husbandry still remains one of the lowest in Europe. The rise in agricultural production was chiefly due to an expansion of the area under cultivation, soil improvement, greater mechanization and better farming methods.

DIAGRAM 1

Growth of agricultural output

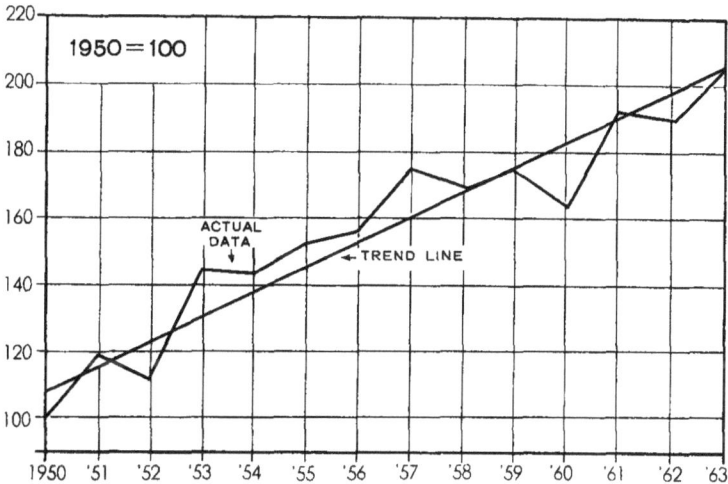

The area of cultivated land has increased from 2.8 million hectares before the war to about 3.7 million hectares in recent years. This expansion resulted mainly from the almost complete elimination of fallow and the extension of cultivation upon the mountain slopes. Irrigation projects have played an important part in the contribution made by land improvement to agricultural development. Although the irrigated area increased by some 70 per cent over the period 1950-1963, the 450 thousand hectares of irrigated

29

land are still too limited, if we bear in mind that the total irrigable area is estimated at one million hectares.

TABLE 3

Composition of crop production during the period 1952–1963
(Four-year average percentage at 1954 prices)

Categories of crop products	1952–55	1956–59	1960–63
I. Agricultural products exclusively for domestic consumption of which	46.7	45.8	42.4
(i) Wheat	(19.9)	(21.5)	(19.2)
(ii) Olive oil	(8.6)	(9.0)	(8.6)
(iii) Edible pulse	(2.6)	(2.4)	(2.4)
II. Animal feed	16.8	16.1	17.0
III. Traditional exportable products of which	17.2	16.7	16.1
(i) Tobacco	(10.7)	(11.3)	(10.6)
(ii) Currants and raisins	(3.8)	(3.7)	(3.6)
IV. New exportable products[a] of which	19.3	21.4	24.5
(i) Cotton	(5.7)	(6.8)	(8.6)
(ii) Citrus fruits, apples, peaches	(3.0)	(4.0)	(4.9)
Total	100.0	100.0	100.0

a Including the total output of products which were first exported after the war, even in small quantities
Sources: Ministry of Agriculture, Bank of Greece.

Another factor conducive to increased agricultural production during the 1950–1963 period was the substantial extension of mechanization. Yet, although the number of tractors in use increased over fourfold during the period under review, there would still seem to be considerable margins for expanding agricultural mechanization. As regards improved farming methods, the introduction of better seeds (particularly for wheat and cotton) and an increased use of fertilizers have played an important part.

In spite of the efforts made throughout the postwar period, there is still inadequate progress towards an extensive development of Greek agriculture through an increase in the output of products which satisfy current trends in world demand. The composition of agricultural production has not undergone any substantial change, and the rise in agricultural output during recent years concentrated mainly on products consumed by the home market. As can be seen from Table 3, these products (categories I, II) made up about 60 per cent of the total volume of agricultural output.

The promotion of agriculture is hindered by certain specific obstacles inherent to the structure of primary production. Productivity increases depend on the attitude of the numerous economic units responsible for production; and their adjustment to a program and the objectives of economic policy is made all the more difficult by the low educational level of the farming population. The problem is particularly acute in countries like Greece, where small farming lots are prevalent and there is a considerable shortage of arable land.

THE INDUSTRIAL SECTOR

During the period under review, industrial production increased at an average annual rate of about 7.5 per cent. This rate compares favorably with industrial expansion in most countries of Europe over the same period. Despite this increase, the share of the manufacturing sector in the total gross national product still remains low (18.7 per cent in 1963 as compared to 17 per cent in 1950–1951).

Development has not taken place at a uniform rate in the various branches of the industrial sector during the period under review. Production of building materials, paper, electric appliances, and chemicals increased at a high rate

31

whereas output of foodstuffs and textiles—the two largest industries in Greece—rose at a slower rate than the general index of industrial production.

TABLE 4

Growth of industrial output in selected countries

Countries	Annual rates of growth			Percentage share of manufacturing in G.D.P. at constant prices[a]	
	1950–55	1956–63	1950–63	1950	1962
Argentina	2.2	–2.0	0.4	23.4	22.3
Belgium	5.3	4.4	4.7	30.0	32.4
W.Germany	13.0	6.2	8.8	36.3	45.4
GREECE	10.2	5.7	7.5	16.9	19.6
France	7.1	6.9	7.0	36.1	38.0
India	6.7	7.0	6.9	16.7	17.2
Italy	8.8	9.5	9.2	28.6	36.1
Norway	6.4	5.1	5.6	27.7	27.3
United Kingdom	3.8	2.3	2.9	34.9	35.5

[a] These percentages are not strictly comparable owing to differences in valuation, base year etc. See sources cited.

Sources: U.N., *Monthly Bulletin of Statistics* Jan. 1958, 1961, 1963 July 1964. Federation of Greek Industries and National Statistical Service of Greece.
O.E.C.D., *Statistics of National Accounts 1950–1961* and *1955–1962,* Paris 1964.
U.N., *Yearbooks of National Account Statistics 1957* and *1963.*
Ministry of Coordination, *National Accounts of Greece 1948–1959, 1958–1962.*

This differential rate of increase has not succeeded in effecting a sufficient change in the structure of Greek industry, during the period 1950–1963. According to national accounts data, the share of consumer and producer goods

32

in the total value of manufacturing output (at 1954 prices) was 85 and 15 per cent respectively in 1950, the corresponding figures for 1962 being 76 and 24 per cent. Moreover, Greek industry was still mainly oriented towards the domestic market.

DIAGRAM 2

Indices of industrial production in Greece

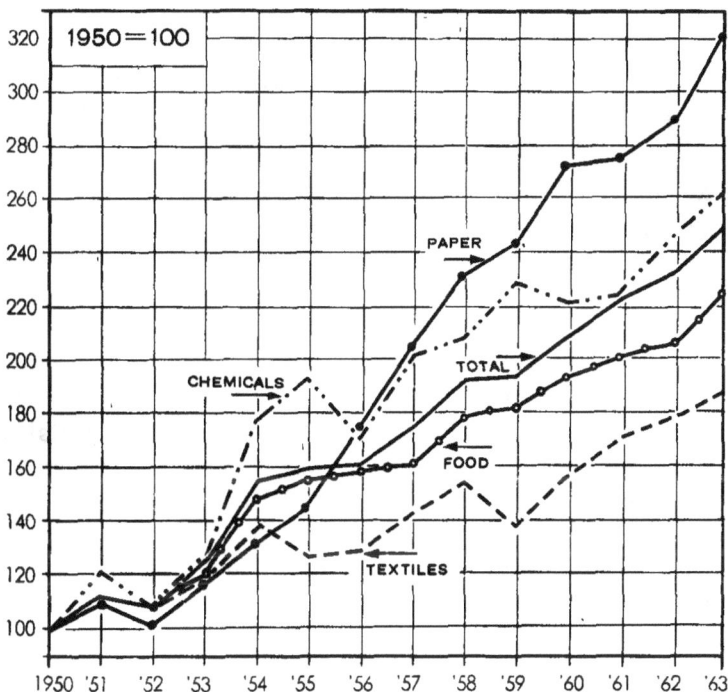

Gross fixed investment in the manufacturing sector as a proportion of total gross investment fell between 1950 and 1961 (from 18.7 to 9.1 per cent respectively) and amounted to only 10.4 per cent in the last five years. This percentage appears to be quite inadequate for a substantial expansion and improvement of industrial capacity and is far below the proportion of investment devoted to the manufacturing

33

sector in advanced economies. Basically these developments reflect the fact that, until recently, the response of entrepreneurs to existing and newly created investment opportunities in the industrial sector was inadequate. Greek industry consists mainly of small units and is characterized by a high degree of regional concentration. Thus, according to a sample of 977 enterprises, taken from the Register of the Industrial Development Corporation, 55 per cent of the total number of industrial units employ less than 100 persons each. On the other hand, data collected through the industrial survey conducted by the National Statistical Service, show that industrial concerns in the Athens-Piraeus area employ 57 per cent of the total number of industrial workers and account for 59 per cent of the total value added by manufacture.

EMPLOYMENT AND LABOR PRODUCTIVITY

Greek employment statistics are rather scanty. Some sufficiently reliable information can, however, be drawn from the censuses of the years 1951 and 1961, suitably adjusted. According to these data, within the decade 1951–1961 total employment increased at an average annual rate of 1.5 per cent, while the rate of increase of the population was only 0.9 per cent. It is worth noting that the rise in employment was accompanied by an even faster increase in the active population (1.7 per cent annually). This leads to the conclusion that, in all probability, the percentage of labor employed did not change significantly throughout the period under review. However, the considerably faster increase in G.D.P. during the same period (annual rate 6.0 per cent) indicates a substantial rise in labor productivity, which is estimated at 4.3 per cent annually. As shown in Table 5, this rate was one of the highest in Europe.

Changes in productivity by sector cannot be analyzed owing to the lack of a sectoral breakdown of employment data.

TABLE 5

Annual rates of increase of output, employment, and output per worker
1950 – 1961

Countries	Rate of increase of G.D.P.	Rate of increase of employment	Rate of increase of G.D.P. per worker
Belgium	2.9d	0.33	2.27d
Britain	2.7	0.74	1.91
W. Germany	7.5	2.03	5.34
GREECE	6.2	0.76a	5.33e
Iceland	4.4	1.59b	2.99f
Italy	6.2	2.07c	4.07c
Netherlands	4.6	1.28	3.42
Norway	3.8	0.21	3.61
Portugal	4.7	0.37b	4.07f

a On the basis of census data for 1951 and 1961
b Average computed on the basis of data for 1950 and 1960
c 1954–1961
d 1953–1961
e 1951–1961
f 1950–1960

Sources: O.E.C.D., *Statistics of National Accounts 1950-1961*, Paris 1964.
O.E.C.D., *Manpower Statistics*, 1950–1962, Paris 1963.

INVESTMENT

The trend of investment activity can best be seen in Table 8, which shows the difference in the average growth rate of investment between the periods 1950–1956 and 1956–1963. The percentage of gross investment to gross domestic product rose from 17.1 in the period 1950–1955 to 25.6 in the period 1956–1961. In spite of this, per capita investment in Greece is still very low in comparison with that of advanced countries, as Table 6 clearly shows.

As regards productivity of investment, the changes in

the incremental capital-output ratio indicate that although productivity decreased substantially between the two periods examined, it still remains one of the highest in Europe.

DIAGRAM 3

Public and private investment
(Billions drachmas, at 1954 prices)

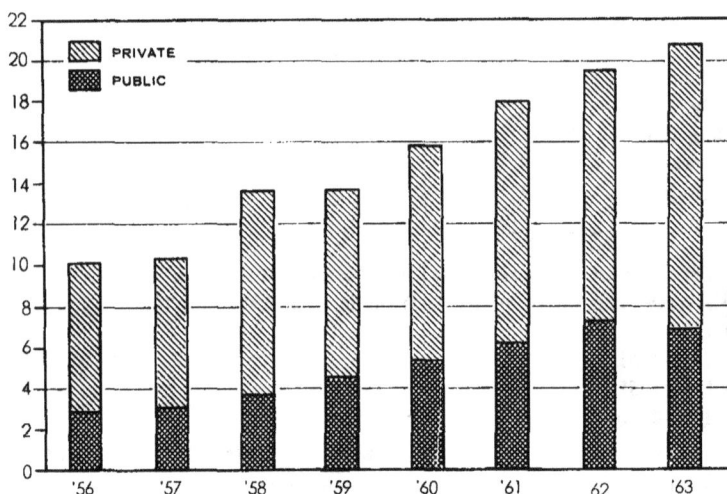

In Greece, investment is neither adequate in quantity nor wholly satisfactory in structure. As can be seen in Table 7, investment in agriculture and industry during the period 1950–1963 absorbed on the average only 25.3 per cent of total investment, while investment in housing amounted to 33.2 per cent of the total. The larger share of investment in housing is connected with the problem of private investment in Greece, discussed in a later chapter, but in part it was also due to the need to reconstruct the buildings destroyed during the enemy occupation, the guerrilla war, and by earthquakes. It should be noted,

36

however, that although the absolute magnitude of investment in housing has increased, it represents a declining percentage of the total.

TABLE 6

Rates of growth of output, investment ratios, incremental capital-output ratios and per capita investment in selected countries, 1950–1961

| Countries | Percentage | | | | | | Per capita gross investment 1954[a] |
| | Average annual rate of growth of gross domestic product at 1954 prices | | Ratio of gross invest. to gross domestic product at 1954 prices | | Incremental capital-output ratio | | |
	1950–55	1956–61	1950–55	1956–61	1950–55	1956–61	1961
Belgium	4.5[b]	2.3	17.5[b]	18.6	3.9[b]	8.1	200
W. Germany	9.0	6.3	23.3	26.9	2.6	4.3	275
GREECE	6.5	6.0	17.1	25.6	2.6	4.3	71
Italy	6.3	6.1	21.2	25.0	3.4	4.1	148
Netherlands	5.4	4.0	23.4	26.5	4.3	6.6	200
Norway	3.7	3.8	31.8	31.8	8.6	8.4	318
Portugal	5.3[c]	5.2	15.6[c]	18.5	2.9[c]	3.6	50

[a] At 1954 prices, in U. S. dollars
[b] 1953–1955
[c] 1952–1955

Sources: O.E.C.D., *Statistics of National Accounts 1950–1961*, Paris 1964. U.N., *Monthly Bulletin of Statistics*, April 1964. I.M.F., *International Financial Statistics*, August 1962.

Investment in the agricultural sector increased its share in total investment during the period examined, whereas the share of industrial investment declined substantially, from 19 per cent in 1950–1952 to 11.4 per cent in 1962–1963.

As shown in Table 8, public investment between 1950 and 1963 increased at an average annual rate of 6.1 per cent. In the last two years of the period its share in total investment amounted to 35 per cent.

TABLE 7

Breakdown of fixed capital formation by sector of economic activity
(excluding ships, at 1954 prices)

	1950–52	1953–55	1956–58	1959–61	1962–63	1950–63 average
Agriculture	11.6	7.9	11.6	16.5	13.8	12.2
Industry	19.0	11.7	13.3	9.5	11.4	13.1
Power, water supply, transport, communications etc.	27.1	22.0	25.2	30.1	29.5	26.6
Housing	25.9	41.2	36.2	30.5	31.2	33.2
Other	16.4	17.2	13.7	13.4	14.1	14.9
Total	100.0	100.0	100.0	100.0	100.0	100.0

Source: Ministry of Coordination, *Investment in Greece in the Postwar Period,* Athens 1964.

The investment effort of the public sector was mainly focused on transport, electrification, and land improvement, but an increasing interest has also been shown in the promotion of industrial projects.

TABLE 8

Average annual changes in gross fixed capital formation
(excluding ships, at constant 1954 prices)

	Average 1950–1956	Average 1956–1963	Average 1950–1963
Private investment	+8.5	+10.3	+9.5
Public investment	—2.4	+13.3	+6.1
Total investment	+4.0	+11.1	+7.8

Source: *Greek National Accounts 1948-1959* and *1958-1962.* Figures for 1963 are provisional estimates.

PRICES

Between 1950 and 1963, the average annual rates of increase in wholesale and consumer prices were 5.5 and 4.9 per cent respectively. It is more instructive, however, to divide the period from 1950 to 1963 into two phases, namely the phase of inflation (up to 1956) and that of gradual price stabilization (1956 onwards).

TABLE 9

Percentage annual changes in prices during the 1950–1963 period

	Consumer price index[a]	Wholesale price index
1950–1951	+12.6	+21.2
1951–1952	+ 5.1	— 0.7
1952–1953	+ 9.0	+15.3
1953–1954	+15.1	+12.1
1954–1955	+ 5.8	+ 7.3
1955–1956	+ 3.6	+ 8.6
1950–1956 (average)	+ 8.5	+10.6
1956–1957	+ 2.3	+ 0.6
1957–1958	+ 1.4	— 2.4
1958–1959	+ 2.3	+ 1.6
1959–1960	+ 1.6	+ 2.3
1960–1961	+ 1.8	+ 1.6
1961–1962	— 0.3	— 0.9
1962–1963	+ 3.0	+ 5.1
1956–1963 (average)	+ 1.7	+ 1.1
1950–1963	+ 4.9	+ 5.5

a Data for 1950–1959 are based on the cost-of-living index. After 1959 the calculations refer to data from the consumer price index for Greek urban centers

Sources: Bank of Greece, National Statistical Service of Greece.

The first phase, which extends from 1950 through to 1956, is characterized by pronounced upward price movements far in excess of world trends. Businessmen and the general public exhibited during this period great sensitivity to price rises and this attitude, influenced decisively by the psychology of inflation, is especially reflected in substantial hoardings of gold sovereigns, low propensity to invest in productive projects, greater preference for investment in housing and a reluctance to bank deposits. Within this phase, a further distinction should be made between the years before 1953 and those from 1953 to 1956. Although the latter period

DIAGRAM 4

The course of prices, 1950–1963
1950=100

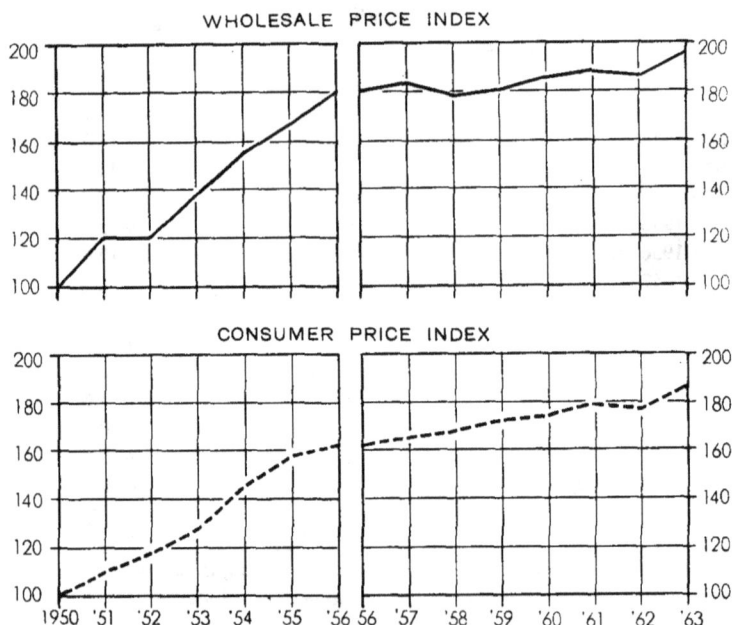

WHOLESALE PRICE INDEX

CONSUMER PRICE INDEX

1950 '51 '52 '53 '54 '55 '56 56 '57 '58 '59 '60 '61 '62 '63

was characterized by a substantial rise in prices, mainly attributable to the devaluation of the drachma by 50 per cent in April 1953 (from 15 drs=1 U.S. $ to 30 drs=1 U.S. $), it was also the starting point for a qualitative differentiation

40

of inflationary forces, which finally led to the end of the inflationary phase, as discussed in detail in Chapter Five.

The second phase, which began towards the end of 1956, is the phase of relative monetary stability. During this phase price increases were much lower than in most European countries, as can be seen in Table 10.

TABLE 10

Average annual changes in consumer and wholesale prices
in selected countries during the 1956–1963 period

Countries	Consumer price index	Wholesale price index
Finland	4.9	3.8
France	5.7	4.7
W. Germany	2.2	0.7
GREECE	1.7	1.1
Italy	2.9	0.7
Netherlands	3.0	0.3
Norway	3.0	1.0
Spain	7.0	6.1
Sweden	3.4	1.2
Switzerland	2.1	0.7
United Kingdom	2.5	1.7[a]
U.S.A.	1.7	0.6

[a] Index for finished manufactured goods

Source: U.N., *Monthly Bulletin of Statistics*, April 1964.

At the same time, a fundamental change took place in the attitude of the public, which gradually recovered from the psychology of inflation. This change was marked by a reduced tendency to hoard gold and by willingness to deposit funds with the banks. From about mid-1956 onwards bank deposits started increasing at a fast rate and the dependence of the commercial banks on the central bank in meeting the credit needs of the economy gradually diminished. Normal credit conditions were thus restored and there was a reduction in loan transactions outside the banking system. (During the preceding period, there had been a great increase in such transactions, mainly caused by the severe shortage of funds in the organized money market.)

THE BALANCE OF PAYMENTS

At the beginning of the period under review, Greece's annual deficit on current account was of the order of $226 million (1950–1952 average), representing about 58 per cent of total

DIAGRAM 5

Balance of payments on current account
(in millions U. S. dollars)

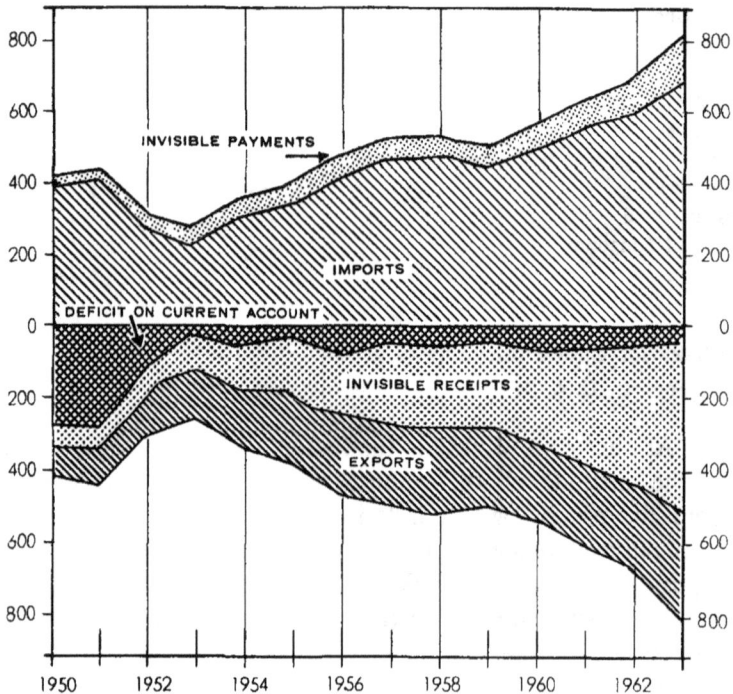

42

foreign exchange expenditure, and was covered largely by U.S. aid. Recently, this deficit has been of the order of $70 million (1961–1963 average), representing 10 per cent of foreign exchange expenditure, and has been covered mainly from capital inflow. The reduction in the deficit on current account was accompanied by a rise in foreign exchange reserves from $54 million in 1950 to $278 million in 1963. It is worth noting, however, that short-term liabilities to foreigners, mainly in the form of suppliers' credits, have also increased substantially during the same period.

TABLE 11

Trade deficit and deficit on current account
(in millions U.S. dollars)

	Trade deficit	Deficit on current account
1950	309.2	278.8
1951	324.1	287.1
1952	162.1	113.3
1953	102.0	17.6
1954	158.6	64.5
1955	145.5	27.7
1956	231.1	87.9
1957	252.3	66.3
1958	248.7	78.8
1959	242.3	60.0
1960	288.5	80.8
1961	326.9	83.4
1962	365.9	73.9
1963	412.5	56.1

Source: Bank of Greece, Foreign Exchange Statistics.

The gradual improvement in the balance of payments began in 1953, when the Greek currency was devalued. After this year, Greek exports showed a temporary upswing, while invisible receipts increased at a rapid pace, to become an important factor in the establishment and maintenance of internal and external monetary equilibrium.

Although the balance of payments improved considerably between 1950 and 1963, structural weaknesses still render the country's foreign trade position delicate. This can be seen in Table 12 by comparing the deficits on current account of Greece with those of selected countries since 1950.

TABLE 12

Deficit on current account as a percentage of gross national income at market prices in selected countries
(Surpluses $= +$, deficits $= -$)

	1950	1956	1962
Belgium	— 2.7	+2.0	+ 0.2
France	+ 0.7	—1.3	+ 0.6
W. Germany	— 1.2	+3.4	+ 1.0
GREECE	—18.2	—8.9	—10.6
Italy	— 0.7	—1.2	—
Netherlands	— 5.8	—2.2	+ 1.7
Portugal	— 4.4	—4.4	—11.8a

a 1961

Sources: *Greek National Accounts 1948-1959, 1958-1962.*
O.E.C.D., *Bulletin Général de Statistiques,* 1961, 1963 No 12.
I.F.S., February 1963.
O.E.C.D., *Statistiques Générales,* November 1962.

Apart from the widening gap in Greece's foreign trade, which reflects the country's limited export capacity and rapidly rising imports, the Greek balance of payments presents as yet another structural weakness. It still depends —though to a smaller degree than at the beginning of the period under review—on capital inflow in the form of private or government unilateral transfers.

II

MONETARY AND CREDIT POLICY, 1950—1963

INTRODUCTION

Monetary and credit policy, especially since the mid-fifties, has been based on the view that monetary stability and economic development should not be seen as two independent policy objectives, each of which could be pursued separately. The basic assumption has always been that monetary stability cannot be maintained in the longer run in a stagnant economy and that satisfactory rates of growth cannot be maintained steadily in an environment of monetary instability.

The monetary authorities have fully recognized the legitimate aspiration of the Greek people for higher living standards and have geared their policies towards the target of rapid development. Moreover, the need to preserve monetary stability as a necessary condition for growth has been interpreted in a relative sense and within the limits set by international price movements and the psychological reactions of the public. Monetary stability has never been the sole aim of policy for the simple reason that an attempt on the part of the authorities to maintain monetary stability at all costs would have been futile. In the course of time, such a policy would also inevitably have clashed with the legitimate demands of the people for higher living standards. Nevertheless, in the interests of economic growth, existing inflationary pressures had to be contained within the limits imposed by the psychological attitudes of an inflation-conscious public. Monetary policies sought to control the excess demand arising from unwarranted increases in consumption expenditure which very often resulted in a mounting import bill of luxury goods. On the other hand, efforts on the part of private enterprise or the government to invest in fields conducive to the development of the country were not hindered by lack of funds. On the contrary, quite often funds available for investment were not fully utilized by private enterprise.

The problem of underdevelopment would have ceased to exist long ago if it could be solved by resorting to the printing machine. However, it is equally unreasonable to hold that a state of external and internal monetary stability is a sufficient condition for rapid and sustained development.

A lop-sided and superficial approach to the thorny problem of growth and stability can easily lead to an incorrect evaluation of prevailing conditions and, consequently, to unfounded criticism of the policy adopted. Monetary and credit policies pursued by Greek monetary authorities have been criticized by some as being inflationary and by others as being deflationary. This conflict of opinion shows a certain lack of balance in the criticisms levelled by both sides and provides a valid indication that the right "mix" of policies has in fact been followed by the authorities. Even so, the controversy deserves some analysis and we will, therefore, examine it in more detail.

Some critics, who have described the monetary policy pursued as inflationary, maintain that the achievement of monetary stability has only been illusory and that inflationary pressures have been exported in the form of external deficits.

There is no doubt that even during the second phase of the period under review, there were times when inflationary pressures were intensified and affected adversely the balance of trade. Numerous factors contributed to the inflationary pressures during the period under review. Heavy defense expenditures, the deficit financing of the agricultural sector, and the effort to utilize fully the development potential of the economy, all contributed to a monetary expansion which substantially exceeded the actual increase achieved in production and capacity.

Judging, however, from developments during 1955–1963

46

in the price level and the balance of payments, and the continuous fall in the income velocity of circulation, the monetary authorities appear to have evaluated the movement of real magnitudes correctly and to have allowed monetary expansion to proceed within the safety limits set by the psychological reactions of the public. Nevertheless, it cannot be doubted that one of the basic factors which contributed to the liberalization of monetary policy since 1955 has been the substantial rise in foreign invisible receipts. This favorable trend in invisible receipts not only helped to finance a rising import bill but also made a useful addition to foreign exchange reserves.

It could be pointed out, of course, that monetary policy has not completely eliminated inflationary pressures. The fact is, however, that a price "freeze" has never been the objective of monetary policy. Indeed, such an objective would have been both unattainable and wrong, given the aim of rapid growth and the upward trend in international prices. The aim of policy has always been the maintenance of relative monetary stability by keeping inflationary pressures within the limits set by the psychological reactions of the public and by parallel movements of foreign prices. Within this context of policy priorities, relative monetary stability has been successfully maintained (see Table 10), and growth has proceeded without any obstruction by monetary policy.

As regards the persistent deficit of the trade balance, it should be noted that this is primarily a result of the structural weaknesses of the Greek economy, the elimination of which requires reformative measures that do not fall directly within the sphere of monetary action. If financial policy had restricted monetary and credit magnitudes to the level which would bring the balance of trade to equilibrium, the inevitable result would have been a slowing down of the rate of growth. Generally, the existence of lagging sectors in the development process imposes a short-term dilemma—the choice between an intensification of inflationary pressures and a slowing

47

down of the growth rate. Such a dilemma, however, did not arise in the case of Greece. Despite the substantial deficits on the trade balance (see Table 13), the monetary authorities have fully exploited the leeway afforded by the large surpluses in the balance of invisibles and by capital inflow and have maintained monetary stability without restricting the growth rate of the Greek economy.

Other critics, while recognizing that monetary stability has been successfully maintained, hold that the efforts of the authorities to keep the drachma sound have adversely affected the rate of growth of the Greek economy. Their thesis has been that a more liberal monetary policy would not have led to inflation but to a higher rate of growth, and even that should it, in fact, lead to inflation, the effects on growth would be beneficial.

We think that this line of argument pays little attention to the interdependence between economic development and monetary stability. Long periods of monetary instability and the Greek people's bitter experience with galloping inflation during the war and the immediate postwar years, have made the tolerance limits of the public very narrow.

Quite apart from its impact on resource allocation, a rapid rise in prices at home—which would have been out of line with relative developments abroad—would have created serious difficulties in the balance of payments necessitating the imposition of trade restrictions or possibly a new devaluation. Both measures would have been equally unwelcome in view of the growing tendency towards more liberal arrangements for world trade and payments and the need to avoid unnecessary changes in parities.

The rate of growth of G.N.P. in relation to the rapid rise in the money supply in the 1950's strengthens the view that the pursuit of relative monetary stability has not been an obstacle to the creation of an effective expansionary impulse in the economy, which is reflected in the substantial deficits of the trade balance. Table 14 gives comparative

MONETARY AND CREDIT POLICY

data on money supply and G.N.P. changes in a number of countries including Greece.

TABLE 13

Deficits in the balance of trade, 1950—1963
(in millions U.S. dollars)

1950	—309.2
1951	—324.1
1952	—162.1
1953	—102.0
1954	—158.6
1955	—145.5
1956	—231.1
1957	—252.3
1958	—248.7
1959	—242.3
1960	—288.5
1961	—326.9
1962	—365.5
1963	—412.5

Source: Bank of Greece, Foreign Exchange Statistics.

A substantial part of the expansionary impulses operating on the Greek economy in the 1950's resulted in higher prices and larger current account deficits, as shown in Table 15. Fluctuations in aggregate production mainly reflect the four-year cycle of agricultural production. This is a clear indication that both the rate of growth achieved and its sharp fluctuations were basically influenced by the structural weaknesses of the Greek economy and not by monetary or credit restrictions.

The volume of financing should be adapted to the "absorptive capacity" of a developing country's economy. It appears, however, that the "absorptive capacity" of the Greek economy has not been appraised correctly by those critics who hold that the rate of growth would have been higher if credit and the money supply had expanded at a faster pace. This incorrect appraisal may stem from a misunderstanding of the concept of "absorptive capacity." The concept relates to

49

TABLE 14

Percentage annual changes in G.N.P. and money supply in Greece and in selected countries, 1956–1961

Countries	Increase in money supply (end of period levels)						Increase in G.N.P. at constant prices						Increase in money supply in excess of G.N.P. increase					
	1956	1957	1958	1959	1960	1961	1956	1957	1958	1959	1960	1961	1956	1957	1958	1959	1960	1961
Argentina	15.42	17.21	41.31	43.13	28.34	11.30	-0.86	4.01	2.75	-4.77	4.40	5.56	16.28	13.20	38.56	47.90	23.94	5.65
Austria	4.49	6.63	11.07	10.00	5.49	8.36	5.12	5.88	3.64	2.34	8.91	5.26	-0.63	0.75	7.43	7.66	-3.42	3.10
GREECE	12.84	18.69	9.25	16.24	18.98	14.85	7.00	9.09	2.75	3.77	4.29	12.36	5.84	9.60	6.50	12.47	14.69	2.49
India[a]	6.40	4.25	3.08	7.11	6.48	4.76	1.94	4.87	-0.82	7.06	1.80	7.15	4.46	-0.62	3.90	0.05	4.68	-2.39
Ireland	—	6.98	-0.48	3.64	6.80	6.20	-1.71	0.58	-3.53	4.96	5.78	3.62	1.71	6.40	3.05	-1.32	1.02	2.58
Italy	8.01	5.12	10.72	14.06	13.66	15.68	4.18	6.28	4.40	7.66	7.09	8.01	3.83	-1.16	6.32	6.40	6.57	7.67
Netherlands	-3.65	-1.84	11.92	4.54	6.70	7.69	3.44	2.98	-0.06	5.04	8.27	2.64	-7.09	-4.82	11.98	-0.50	-1.57	5.50
Portugal	6.54	5.82	7.46	8.94	6.16	0.64	4.16	4.41	1.39	5.83	8.13	7.66	2.38	1.41	6.07	3.11	-1.97	-7.02
Turkey[b]	25.28	22.59	6.88	14.02	10.89	7.64	6.80	6.32	11.80	4.40	2.39	-0.51	18.48	16.27	-4.92	9.62	8.50	8.15

[a] Net domestic product at factor cost   [b] Gross domestic product at factor cost

Sources: 1. *International Financial Statistics*, Oct. 1963.
2. *Yearbook of National Accounts Statistics*, 1962.

TABLE 15

Analysis of the expansionary impulses in the Greek economy, 1950-1963
(in billions drachmas at current prices)

	1950	1951	1952	1953	1954	1955	1956	1957	1958	1959	1960	1961	1962	1963[a]
I. Previous year's production	25.7	28.8	35.9	37.9	50.3	58.7	66.6	77.7	83.3	87.5	90.6	97.0	110.1	117.6
II. Current year's National Expenditure (A+B)	33.8	40.1	40.7	52.8	62.0	69.4	81.9	88.2	93.0	95.2	102.4	115.8	124.2	137.4
A. Consumption	27.8	33.6	35.9	45.5	54.6	59.5	69.7	74.2	77.5	79.5	85.3	93.9	100.4	110.7
B. Investment	6.0	6.5	4.8	7.3	7.4	9.9	12.2	14.0	15.5	15.7	17.1	21.9	23.8	26.7
III. Expansionary impulses (II−I=C+D)	8.1	11.3	4.8	14.9	11.7	10.7	15.3	10.5	9.2	7.7	11.8	18.8	14.1	19.8
C. Increase in production	—	2.7	—	5.5	1.9	4.6	4.7	7.1	2.3	3.3	3.9	12.0	5.0	9.1
D. Excess Demand (1+2)	8.1	8.6	4.8	9.4	9.8	6.1	10.6	3.4	6.9	4.4	7.9	6.8	9.1	10.7
1. Increase in prices	3.1	4.4	2.0	6.8	6.4	3.3	6.4	-1.0	1.3	-0.2	2.5	1.2	2.6	4.3
2. Current account deficit[b]	5.0	4.2	2.8	2.6	3.4	2.8	4.2	4.4	5.6	4.6	5.4	5.6	6.5	6.4

[a] Provisional estimates

[b] Emigrant remittances have not been included in the current account and consequently the deficit is larger than the one given in Table 48. Another reason for the discrepancy is that the above figures are based on customs statistics whereas those in Table 48 are based on foreign exchange statistics

Sources: *National Accounts of Greece*, O.E.E.C. *Statistics of Sources and Uses of Finance.*

the capacity of a given economy to utilize productively the available capital resources and not to its ability to use funds indiscriminately for any type of spending. Indeed, if the concept were given this meaning, then the "absorptive capacity" of low-income countries would be almost limitless. Consequently, an attempt to relate the credit and money volume to the "absorptive capacity" (as defined by the critics) of a developing economy would not only be futile as a means of promoting productive utilization of resources but would finally end up in galloping inflation.

The monetary and credit policies pursued have always exhausted and often exceeded the limits of the Greek economy's aggregate productive capacity. The aim has always been to raise total effective demand for investment and consumption somewhat above total supply so as to exercize a lasting expansionary influence on the economy. Whenever private and public investment tended to decline, monetary and credit measures were introduced to stimulate consumer expenditure, which in any case tended to increase autonomously. The effort to influence total effective demand in the direction of more productive activities has in no case restricted consumer expenditure to an extent likely to create a lag in total effective demand, as compared with the productive potential of the economy as a whole. Higher consumption, either as an expansionary factor or as a socioeconomic goal, has never been underscored. On the other hand, demand for investment has been accorded—as in all developing countries—a high priority rating. As long as inflationary pressures resulting from increasing consumption did not assume dangerous dimensions (owing to an expansion in aggregate supply or a drop in the demand for investment) a faster rate of increase in consumption was both desirable and, of course, easily attained.

It would be useful at this stage to consider in some detail the meaning of the term "absorptive capacity." This will also allow us to consider the extent to which

52

monetary and credit policy assisted in the productive utilization of resources during the period under review.

In a mature and balanced economy a profitable line of business activity can in principle be considered as socially useful except where it leads to a monopolistic situation which is considered to be undesirable on broader policy considerations. Even in advanced countries, however, economic policy favors some sectors of the economy that are considered of special significance to social and economic aims.

TABLE 16

Absorption of commercial bank funds earmarked for long-term finance of industry (in millions drachmas)

		Funds earmarked for long-term finance of industry	Loans extended for long-term industrial investment	Idle commercial bank funds [a]
1958 :	June	661	65	596
	December	834	136	698
1959 :	June	952	211	741
	December	1,210	250	960
1960 :	June	1,571	346	1,225
	December	1,661	489	1,172
1961 :	June	1,840	665	1,175
	December	2.052	792	1,260
1962 :	June	2,368	850	1,518
	December	2,649	1,139	1,510
1963 :	June	3,069	1,375	1,694
	December	3,364	1,589	1,775

[a] In 1960 banks were allowed to use surplus funds in granting medium-term loans or investing them in treasury bills

Source: Bank of Greece.

In developing countries, however, it is the contribution to the development effort—and not sheer profitability—which

53

provides the basic criterion in judging whether a given line of activity is socially desirable. Since the price mechanism is an inadequate guide to socially productive resource allocation, the authorities are obliged to take those measures which will ensure the most productive use of available resources. Thus, the monetary authorities in Greece enacted policies having as an objective to channel available capital funds into the most productive sectors of the economy. In fact it can be maintained that capital funds thus oriented exceeded the absorptive capacity of the economy.

TABLE 17

Loans granted by Economic Development Financing Organization (E.D.F.O.) and funds left idle
(in millions drachmas)

	Loans to industry and mining for fixed investment (New loans within the year)	Other loans	Idle funds a
1956	380	52	81
1957	83	33	171
1958	111	183	153
1959	140	116	218
1960	38	150	315
1961	74	132	378
1962	292	179	242
1963	276	132	252

a Deposits at the Bank of Greece and holdings of treasury bills. These funds were earmarked for long-term financing of industry, but remained idle due to inadequate demand
Source: Bank of Greece.

The reasons which caused capital funds to be left idle are to be found in the structural weaknesses of the Greek economy—still the main bottleneck to the development effort. Moreover, without underestimating the importance of capital, it appears that in general the scarcity of entrepreneurial talent, of organizational ability and skilled labor which characterizes both private and public sectors in developing economies is the more serious bottleneck to the development effort.

The elimination of these bottlenecks can only be effected through the organization of productive activity, under new forms of effective incentives and, chiefly, through improvements in technical and vocational training. We lay special stress on technical education because it is often not accorded the priority it deserves in development programs.

The monetary authorities have often called attention to similar structural weaknesses in the Greek economy and have made a number of suggestions for improving the standard of technical education and for mobilizing private enterprise. Moreover, they have repeatedly suggested the establishment of effective incentives for industry and the substitution of state initiative for private enterprise in sectors where the latter has been unable or unwilling to undertake investment. Although many of these suggestions have been acted on (e. g., the Industrial Development Corporation, set up in 1960), their effectiveness has very often been limited by the organizational deficiencies of the public sector.

If, despite the structural weaknesses of the Greek economy, the monetary authorities had pursued a more expansionary monetary and credit policy, the resulting inflationary increases in income would have led to an excessive rise in consumption,—particularly in conspicuous consumption—and to the encouragement of activities less socially productive.

An objective analysis of developments in the Greek economy since 1950 would lead to the conclusion that the monetary policy pursued was particularly liberal in the satisfaction of credit requirements for development. At the same time, it prevented an inflationary spiral that would have had undesirable social and economic consequences.

SOME SPECIAL PROBLEMS OF MONETARY AND CREDIT POLICY

Introduction

The fundamental task of monetary and credit policy in a developing economy is to provide the greatest possible assistance to the development effort within the necessary environment of monetary equilibrium. In pursuing this general aim the monetary authorities are faced with a number of special problems. The experience of developed economies is of limited usefulness in this respect. Substantial differences in socioeconomic structure and in the degree to which real magnitudes respond to monetary policy, necessitate the formulation of theoretical principles relevant to conditions in underdeveloped countries. Obviously, such a formulation cannot be attempted here. Some observations, however, based on Greek experience and outlined below may perhaps assist a more general theoretical approach.

First, monetary authorities of developing countries are usually faced with conflicting trends in the level of activity in the various sectors of the economy and are consequently prevented from following a single corrective policy. As a rule, the socially most productive sectors are those which show a lag in their development, while the socially least productive sectors tend to overexpand. Consequently, credit policy should be particularly flexible and should evaluate financing requirements according to each sector's contribution to the development effort. Monetary and credit policy in developing countries cannot exert an effective quantitative influence on income if it does not exercize the appropriate qualitative influence on productive activity. Therefore, quite apart from structural imperfections, the traditional monetary instruments employed in advanced economies (e.g., open-market operations, discount-rate adjustments, variable reserve requirements, etc.) would be inadequate in underdeveloped economies. In this connection, it should be stressed that in both developed and underdeveloped economies there is an asymmetry between the restrictive and the expansionary effectiveness of monetary policy. This has also been the experience of Greece in recent years, during which the stimulating effects of monetary measures favorable to highly productive activity have been blunted by the structural weaknesses of the Greek economy.

Second, the institutional imperfections and peculiarities of developing countries limit the effectiveness of monetary and credit instruments and necessitate the introduction of measures to improve the performance of the money and credit mechanism. A characteristic example is the deficient working of the capital market in most developing countries, which in effect precludes an open-market policy and creates considerable difficulties in the financing of long-term investment. In general, the working of the credit mechanism, and particularly of the banks, should be improved in such a way as to allow them to make a more effective contribution to the efforts of the monetary authorities. The banking system could make a substantial contribution to the development effort if the commercial banks recognized that private profitability does not necessarily conflict with the socioeconomic objectives of development and gave effective assistance to private initiative in the industrial sector.

In conclusion, an effective monetary and credit policy in developed and underdeveloped countries requires the existence of an efficient coordinating body through which the central bank will be able to discharge its function as an adviser to the government.

During the period under review, the Greek authorities have made a sustained effort to tackle all these problems.

The development of the capital market

The Greek capital market, little developed in the prewar period, became completely disorganized during the war and

57

postwar years. Its revival after the war was extremely difficult so long as inflationary pressures persisted.

· The reluctance of savers to invest in long-term securities did not disappear with the restoration of confidence in the national currency. Although there was a decline in the propensity to hoard gold and a sudden increase in bank deposits during 1956–1957, savers still showed a disinclination to invest in securities. It should be stressed, however, that the basic cause of this reluctance lay in the lack of attractive securities offered at the stock exchange. Thus, although savers ceased to view bank deposits with disfavor, they continued to show a preference for investment in real estate as offering greater safety. As an inducement to investment in securities the authorities exempted from taxation income from bonds and provided for the inclusion of a dollar clause in newly issued bonds. In addition, company law was amended to provide greater guarantees to minority shareholders and to allow for the introduction of nonvoting shares, as well as the possibility of converting bonds into shares. At the same time banks were given the freedom to grant loans on collateral of securities.

The authorities sought to discourage other forms of investment. Thus, when the savings deposits which had accumulated at the banks began to exceed the needs of short-term finance, interest rates on deposits were lowered to provide an incentive for the public to invest in securities. In addition, the Currency Committee gave permission to a number of public bodies to invest their funds in securities.

Another measure aimed at the strengthening of the money market was the introduction of treasury bills. Besides its importance as a source of funds, this measure was intended to provide investors with a liquid asset of short maturity and the authorities with an additional lever of credit control.

Finally, the establishment of the Industrial Development Corporation was a measure which will indirectly contribute

58

to the development of the capital market. This Corporation seeks out opportunities for productive investment which could be undertaken by Greek firms, either alone or in collaboration with foreign concerns. If necessary, the Corporation itself could establish firms the shares of which would subsequently be sold to private interests. These shares would possess the additional security provided by state participation.

The results, however, of all these efforts have not been satisfactory and the inadequate quantity and quality of securities appears to have been the main factor which discouraged the public from investing through the stock exchange. Thus, despite the creation of the Industrial Development Corporation and the institutional changes that characterized the period, private firms did not show any marked inclination to draw capital from the organized market. On the other hand, the central government and the Public Power Corporation have raised substantial amounts in the capital market since 1957.

The growth in stock exchange transactions and the fact

TABLE 18

New issues of bonds and shares, 1957–1963
(in millions drachmas)

Year	Bonds				Shares			Grand total
	Public Power Corp.	Central govern- ment	Private firms	Total	Banks	Private firms	Total	
1957	90	—	—	90	—	4	4	94
1958	490	—	—	490	—	64	64	554
1959	300	—	—	300	—	7	7	307
1960	580	750	—	1,330	—	51	51	1,381
1961	740	—	—	740	52	87	139	879
1962	500	990	110	1,600	542	50	592	2,192
1963	—	1,500	22	1,522	—	38	38	1,560

Source: Bank of Greece.

that new issues were largely subscribed by the public, indicate an increased interest in financial investment which did not materialize into a larger demand for stock owing to the lack of suitable securities.

TABLE 19

Value of stock exchange transactions, 1957—1963
(in millions drachmas)

Year	Bonds			Shares			Grand total
	Prewar issues	Postwar issues	Total	Banks	Other	Total	
1957	23.5	11.4	34.9	35.9	79.1	115.0	149.9
1958	20.0	52.5	72.5	45.5	55.0	100.5	173.0
1959	62.5	63.3	125.8	44.3	49.2	93.5	219.3
1960	52.9	125.1	178.0	130.8	110.7	241.5	419.5
1961	32.4	256.1	288.5	205.9	186.9	392.8	681.3
1962	40.2	390.7	430.9	184.8	83.9	268.7	699.6
1963	33.8	428.3	462.1	88.7	59.8	148.5	610.6

Source: Bank of Greece, Athens Stock Exchange.

Finally, the contribution of treasury bills to the development of the money market has not been significant, as the bills were mainly taken up by the banks and, to a minor extent, by public entities.

The reorganization of the banking system

The reorganization of the commercial banking system is another problem which has occupied the authorities. It should be stressed that the responsibility and the role of the banks in a developing country are far wider than in a developed economy. Thus the commercial banks in a developing country should see that available credit is channeled to the various sectors of the economy, not only on the basis of each sector's profitability but also with due regard to its social productivity. To the extent that the banks are not inclined to do this, it becomes necessary to impose special controls until the banking system is able to respond effectively to the requirements of economic development.

A rational allocation of available credit would not only assist the development effort but would also promote the banks' own long-term interests, since the misallocation of credit, by retarding the development of the economy, would sooner or later result in a stagnation of bank turnover and profits. Thus, it is in the banks' own interest not only to satisfy the capital needs of development-minded firms but also to seek out opportunities for productive investment whenever private initiative does not display sufficient interest.

In Greece, the commercial banks have a long tradition and are well organized. Consequently, they have both the duty and the ability to act as advisers to private firms and to become a link between Greek and foreign business by promoting fruitful cooperation and assisting the introduction of modern organization and techniques into Greek industry. Commercial banks in Greece have already moved towards this objective.

In their attempt to reorganize the banking system the authorities have had to face a number of problems.

First, an increase in the share-capital and reserves of the commercial banks. The ratio of capital to deposits has traditionally been regarded as an indicator of the strength and safety of banking institutions. In most foreign countries a ratio of 8–10 per cent is the usual practice and in many countries ratios are legally prescribed. In Greece, as a result of the very rapid rise in deposits after 1956, the ratio has fallen to about 6 per cent. In view of the fact that the banks are expected to assume a more active role in the establishment of new enterprises and the long-term financing of industry, it is clear that the capital position of the banks should be strengthened accordingly. The commercial banks have recognized the need for an increase in their capital and

61

some of them have already floated new shares in the capital market.

Second, the problem of commercial bank profits was another question which the authorities had to face during the early part of the period under review. Bank profits before 1956 were narrow, mainly on account of the limited volume of bank advances. The problem persisted after 1956, when in spite of an increasing volume of bank credit, bank profits were compressed as a result of the rise in interest rates on deposits. With the lowering of deposit rates, however, bank profits showed an upward trend after 1957.

Third, the problem of the accurate implementation of credit controls was met by setting up a Bank Loans Supervisory Service under the Currency Committee. This service collects data on the outstanding debt of private firms to each bank and puts them at the disposal of the commercial banks, thereby enabling the latter to check at any time the obligations of their clients to other banks.

The functions of the Currency Committee

During the period under review, monetary and credit policy was formulated by the Currency Committee. This Committee was set up in 1946 and institutionally reorganized as a body in 1951. Its members are the Ministers of Coordination, Finance, Agriculture, Trade, and Industry, and the Governor of the Bank of Greece. Its functions cover monetary, credit and, to a large extent, balance of payments policy. In the postwar period, bodies with broadly similar functions were set up in many countries (France, Italy, Belgium, *et al.*) to meet the increasing need for coordinating monetary and credit measures with general economic policy. The existence of such bodies with wider responsibilities is all the more necessary in less-developed countries, where the problems of accelerating development and maintaining monetary stability require a close cooperation between the monetary authorities and the government.

In the case of Greece, the role of the Currency Committee is more important, in view of the absence of a pre-established legal framework limiting monetary action such as minimum or maximum reserve requirements, ceilings on government borrowing, minimum gold backing for note circulation, etc. It appears that this absence of legal checks makes for a flexible monetary policy. At the same time, however, these conditions render necessary the existence of a collective body such as the Currency Committee, through which the aims of government policy can be reconciled with the requirements of monetary equilibrium and of a sustained development process.

REVIEW OF MONETARY AND CREDIT POLICY, 1950–1963

Control of money supply

The regulation of the money supply in a way which will satisfy the requirements of development and of monetary stability is a particularly hard task. Monetary policy is faced with the lack of a theoretical model of general validity that would provide a basis for determining in advance the required level of currency circulation. In point of fact, while the quantity theory in some cases provides an approach relevant to monetary conditions in the developing economies, it would be a mistake to consider it as being generally valid and capable of providing a basis for monetary control. The rise in productive capacity which is concomitant with the process of development, and the variability of the velocity of circulation create more complex relations between changes in the amount of money and changes in the price level than those postulated by the simple version of the quantity theory. Equally, other theoretical models in which prices and the level of currency circulation are indirectly correlated, mainly through changes in interest rates, cannot be regarded as corresponding to conditions in the less advanced countries, where real and monetary magnitudes have a substantially different structure to that of developed countries. On the other hand, certain peculiarities of underdevelopment, such as the secondary role of checking deposits and the limited capacity of the banks to create money, simplify to a certain extent the control of the currency circulation by the responsible authorities.

Throughout the period under review, the pursuit of monetary policy was complicated by the operation of certain sociopolitical factors that had an expansionary effect on currency circulation, including defense expenditures, financing of the Agricultural Bank and the agricultural price support policy. In spite of the fact that a series of long-term measures mitigated to a certain extent the highly expansionary effect of the last two factors, their influence in the short run was a problem that had to be solved by appropriate adjustments in the other magnitudes determining the volume of money supply.

In applying the policy of controlling the money supply it was constantly necessary to take account not only of fluctuations in productive activity and developments in the balance of payments, but also of more permanent changes of a structural character, e.g. the decline in the income velocity of circulation between 1950 and 1963.

The velocity of circulation decreased continuously, with the gradual restoration of confidence in the national currency, which induced the public to maintain more comfortable margins of liquidity.

The considerable decrease in the velocity of circulation provides an indication that monetary policy was particularly flexible and responded fully to the requirements of the economy. If monetary policy had been definitely restrictive, the velocity of circulation would have increased in order to meet the monetary needs of the economy. Relevant experience abroad shows that with a constant confidence factor,

64

variations in the velocity of circulation chiefly reflect the expansionary or restrictive character of the monetary policy applied.

TABLE 20

Income velocity of circulation

Year	Bank notes		Total means of payment [b]	
	Income velocity	Percentage change over the previous year	Income velocity	Percentage change over the previous year
1950	16.7	—13.0	12.2	—17.0
1951	19.4	+16.2	12.8	+ 4.9
1952	18.1	— 6.7	12.0	— 6.2
1953	18.6	+ 2.8	12.3	+ 2.5
1954	17.2	— 7.5	10.9	—11.4
1955	16.2	— 5.8	10.4	— 4.6
1956	14.6	— 9.9	9.8	— 5.8
1957	13.6	— 6.8	9.4	— 4.1
1958	12.2	—10.3	8.5	— 9.6
1959	11.7	— 4.1	8.0	— 5.9
1960	10.7	— 8.5	7.1	—11.2
1961	10.5	— 1.9	6.9	— 2.8
1962	9.4	—10.5	6.5	— 5.8
1963[a]	9.0	— 4.3	6.3	— 3.1

[a] Provisional data
[b] Currency in circulation plus sight deposits
   Sources: Bank of Greece, Ministry of Coordination, *National Accounts.*

The liberal line followed by monetary policy in the period under review is also indicated by comparative data of percentage increases in money supply and national income during the past thirteen years. These are shown in Table 21.

The average annual rate of increase in the means of payment was 22.3 per cent in the five years from 1951 to 1955, and 16.0 per cent in the eight years from 1956 to 1963. These rates were very high, not only during the initial period of monetary instability, but also during the subsequent period, which was characterized by a satisfactory degree of monetary stability.

TABLE 21

Percentage changes in money supply and national income, 1951—1963

Year	Increase in bank note circulation (average levels)	Increase in means of payment (average levels)	Increase in national income at constant prices	Increase in bank notes beyond rise in income	Increase in means of payment beyond rise in income
1951	7.37	18.64	9.42	-2.05	9.22
1952	13.41	12.54	-0.07	13.48	12.61
1953	28.55	30.24	14.56a	13.99	15.68
1954	26.84	31.48	3.77	23.07	27.71
1955	19.91	18.55	7.89	12.02	10.66
1956	29.94	24.37	7.00	22.94	17.37
1957	15.80	12.03	9.09	6.71	2.94
1958	16.49	16.02	2.75	13.74	13.27
1959	7.43	9.48	3.77	3.66	5.71
1960	17.04	20.63	4.29	12.75	16.34
1961	16.45	16.87	12.36	4.09	4.51
1962	19.08	13.95	4.51	14.57	9.44
1963	15.97	14.82	7.77b	8.20	7.05

a The drachma was devalued by 50 per cent in that year
b Provisional data

Sources: Bank of Greece, Ministry of Coordination, *National Accounts*.

The increase in money supply beyond the rise in real national income showed wide fluctuations from year to year throughout the 1956–1963 period. These fluctuations are connected with the regulatory action of monetary policy, which sought to adapt currency circulation to the changing requirements of the economy.

The policy of channeling savings into the banks

Until 1955, the reluctance of the public to deposit their savings with the banks was one of the most serious consequences of wartime hyperinflation and postwar inflation.

The continuous depreciations of the Greek currency made bank deposits unprofitable and savers sought safety in hoarding gold sovereigns or risked lending in the unofficial money market, attracted by the high interest rates prevailing in it.

The shortage of commercial bank funds had an inflationary effect as it made necessary the financing of the economy through monetary expansion. At the same time, the fact that the largest part of available savings were utilized outside the normal financial channels and in nonproductive investment from the socioeconomic point of view, rendered more difficult the task of promoting economic development.

The accumulation of deposits in the banks was, therefore, an indispensable condition for restoring monetary stability and stimulating economic development. Monetary policy took this direction as soon as the economic climate had somewhat improved and made possible the restoration of a normal attitude towards bank deposits. After the price level adjustments which followed the currency devaluation of 1953, a trend towards price stability began to appear, accompanied by increasing confidence in the national currency and a slackening in the tendency to hoard gold sovereigns. Under these improved circumstances, it became possible to attract savings into the banks by raising interest rates—an attractive incentive, as savers no longer risked losing either interest or capital (or both) as a result of inflation. In May 1956, the interest rate on savings and time deposits was raised from 7 to 10 per cent with substantial and immediate effect, as can be seen from the fact that by the end of 1956, savings deposits had more than trebled and that their upward trend has been maintained. This development was accompanied by an increase in the number of deposit accounts from 168,520 at the end of 1955 to 1,394,000 at the end of 1963.

Another indication of the radical change in the savers' attitude is provided by the fact that the successive reductions

since 1957 in interest rates on bank deposits have not stopped
the latter's upward trend. This can be seen clearly in Diagram 6, which shows the movement of interest rates and
the course of deposits since 1953.

TABLE 22

Private deposits with commercial banks and special credit institutions
(in millions drachmas)

End of year	Total	Sight	Savings	Time	Blocked
1951	901	697	69	6	129
1952	992	748	82	10	152
1953	1,579	1,175	141	17	246
1954	2,250	1,608	298	38	306
1955	3,102	2,093	523	72	414
1956	4,319	1,898	1,757	227	437
1957	7,611	2,289	4,102	624	596
1958	10,032	2,460	5,771	1,105	696
1959	13,627	2,928	8,543	1,273	883
1960	16,632	3,462	10,835	1,137	1,198
1961	19,722	3,846	12,863	1,479	1,534
1962	24,733	4,109	15,526	3,542	1,556
1963	30,649	4,447	19,824	4,736	1,642

Source: Bank of Greece.

The gradual reduction of interest rates on deposits
was one of the measures adopted by the monetary authorities when it became clear that this step would not endanger
the favorable attitude towards bank deposits. The objectives
were, first, to reduce the cost of money and second, to
strengthen the capital market by attracting to it a portion
of the savings entering the money market. By differentiating
interest rates according to the category of deposits involved,
the authorities sought to favor time deposits in order to
improve bank liquidity and create wider margins for
long-term financing. Time deposits started rising at a rapid
pace in 1962 and now represent about 15 per cent of total
bank deposits compared with an average of 8 per cent up
to 1961.

DIAGRAM 6

Deposits with commercial banks and changes in deposit rates

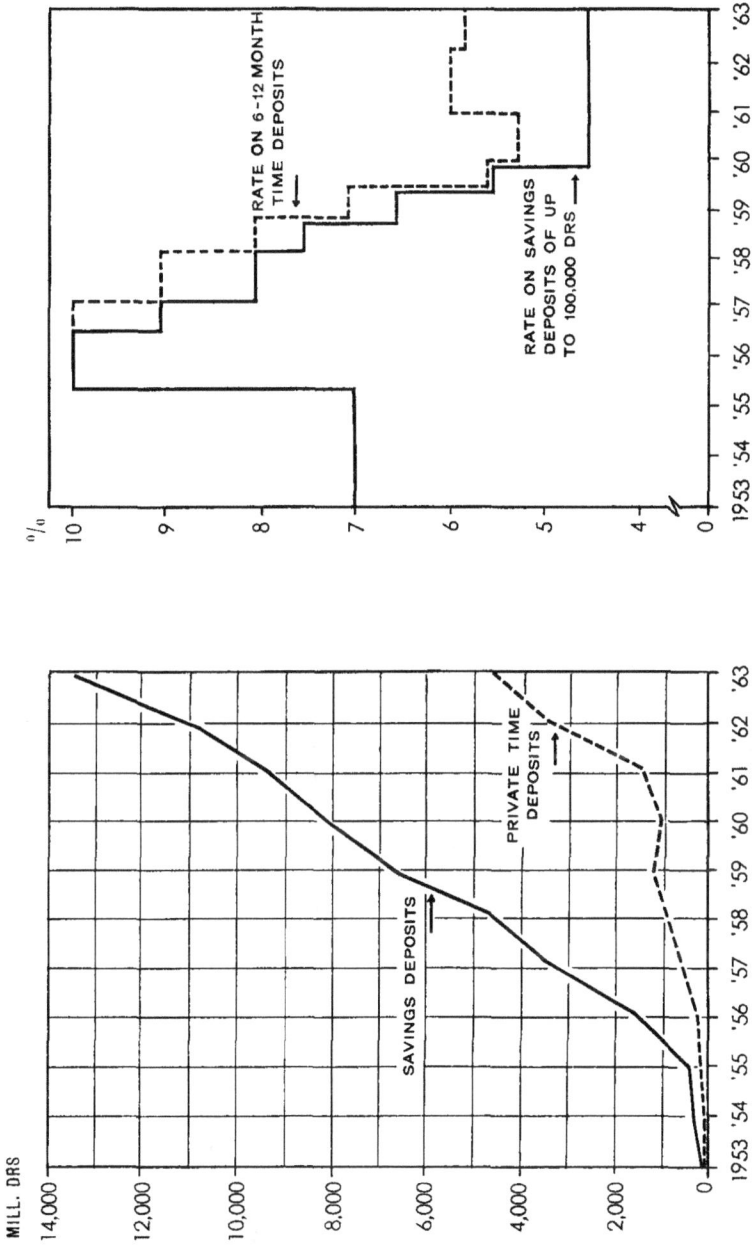

69

TABLE 23

Structure of private deposits
(percentage of total)

End of year	Sight	Savings	Time	Blocked
1955	67	17	2	14
1956	44	41	5	10
1957	30	54	8	8
1958	25	57	11	7
1959	21	63	9	7
1960	21	65	7	7
1961	19	65	8	8
1962	17	63	14	6
1963	15	65	15	5

Source: Bank of Greece.

Policy on the gold sovereign

It is generally true that during prolonged periods of severe inflation and political unrest a substantial part of private savings is directed to gold hoarding, as the best and safest means of safeguarding purchasing power. This is a widespread phenomenon which is not directly related to a particular stage of economic development. Similar trends have been observed during periods of unrest in many advanced countries. In France, for instance, to the present day the central bank systematically intervenes in the gold market and particularly in the market for napoleons.

In Greece, the gold sovereign became the chief means of hoarding during the enemy occupation, when galloping inflation prevailed and the social and economic order was completely disrupted. The public's preference for hoarding gold sovereigns continued through the period of guerrilla warfare and the subsequent years of inflation. Under these conditions, savings could not be attracted to the banks. The gradual elimination of the habit of hoarding gold was necessary if the efforts to develop the capital market were to be successful.

A further reason which made it imperative for the monetary authorities to intervene in the gold market was the great sensitivity shown by the public to changes in the price of the gold sovereign, especially in the early part of the period.

After 1956, official policy regarding the gold sovereign followed a different pattern. During the preceding period, the Bank of Greece had only intervened to restrain rises in the price of the gold sovereign. Since 1956, the aim of intervention has been to keep the price of the gold sovereign close to international levels. To this end, the Bank of Greece bought and sold through authorized dealers any amount of gold sovereigns supplied or demanded at, or around, the "normal" price. The fact that no fixed price was determined in advance introduced a substantial element of risk into speculation on gold which, among other factors, led to a considerable decline in speculative trading in the gold market.

The purchase of gold sovereigns during periods of excessive supply made possible an increase in Bank of Greece gold reserves. Secondly, it prevented the illegal outflow of gold sovereigns abroad, which would inevitably have ensued if the price had been allowed to fall under the pressure of increased supply. On the other hand, the increased stock of gold sovereigns of the Bank of Greece enabled it to intervene effectively whenever hoarding tendencies revived temporarily under the influence of international political crises. In recent years, this policy has made it possible for the Bank of Greece to absorb a considerable proportion of the gold sovereigns hoarded in previous periods.

CREDIT POLICY

General remarks

The main aim of the credit policy applied since 1956 has been to promote the development effort by mitigating the quantitative and qualitative defects of financing which are characteristic of less advanced economies. This wider role of credit policy arises from the need to promote economic growth, rather than from the objective of achieving monetary stability. One of the features of a less advanced economy is the disparity between social productivity and private profitability. This disparity necessitates a discriminatory adjustment of credit to the financing requirements of particular sectors of the economy, on the basis of their contribution to the development process.

The need for this adjustment was the main consideration in formulating credit policy, especially during the second phase of the period under review. More specifically, credit policy was based on the following principles: (1) the provision of ample credit means, even including deficit financing, for productive activities conducive to development; (2) the need to exercize control over the tendency of socially less productive activities and consumer expenditure to over-expand; (3) the reduction of the cost of money in general and the adjustment of interest rates to the special conditions of the sectors to be financed; and (4) the recognition of the need to secure credit means for long-term financing.

The credit policy applied during the period under review neither aimed at, nor did it actually cause a slow-down in the rate of economic development. A proof of this, is the fact that the demand for credit for productive purposes as a rule fell short of available funds. Generally speaking, the credit policy adopted during this period never restricted development in order to serve other purposes, such as monetary stability interpreted in the narrow sense of the term. On the contrary, the authorities were willing to allow more liberal financing of growth-promoting sectors, provided that a corresponding absorptive capacity existed and that relative monetary stability was not jeopardized. Indeed, the main purpose of the controls imposed was to secure adequate credit and thereby channel a larger portion of available resources in the top priority productive sectors of the economy.

Credit policy could not be based solely or chiefly on general quantitative controls under the conditions prevailing in the Greek economy both during the period of inflation and thereafter, when relative monetary stability was attained. Obviously, it was impossible to pursue such a policy during the period of inflation when the economy's credit needs were met largely through central bank advances. However, even when the deposits accumulated in the commercial banks were sufficient to provide the main source of credit, a policy of general quantitative credit control would have been neither adequate nor suitable in a country where qualitative control of economic activity is rendered necessary by the existence of certain tendencies characteristic of underdeveloped economies. The leakage of credit towards consumption and sectors that do not promote growth would have been unavoidable, in view of the high propensity to consume, (especially luxuries), the prevailing trend towards investment in real estate, and the preference for speculative activities in general.

Conditions during the period under review also made it impossible to undertake open market operations, which have no practical significance in countries where a capital market is either nonexistent or insufficiently developed. For this reason Greek monetary policy has never—even before the last war—relied on open-market practices. Similar reasons have prevented the discount-rate mechanism from operating. In consequence, special quantitative and qualitative controls were the main instruments used to give effect to credit policy. Banking regulations have been continuously adjusted to new developments and at the same time a systematic effort has been made to place the banking system on a sound basis and restore the normal role of the banks in the economy. The regulations recently established by the Currency Committee have already simplified credit controls and have transferred a considerable part of the responsibility for sound financing to the commercial banks.

73

General credit controls

Compulsory deposits with central bank—Variable reserve requirements are a routine tool of credit control, and are often employed in advanced economies. This weapon can be equally effective in underdeveloped economies, where other credit-influencing instruments such as the discount rate and open-market policy, are inoperative. Through the proper adjustment of reserve requirements, the monetary authority can bring about an increase or decrease in the liquidity of commercial banks and, therefore, in their ability to expand credit. At the same time these compulsory deposits provide a means whereby the central bank can pursue special credit policy aims and promote the distribution of credit according to development criteria.

During the period under review, Greek commercial banks were obliged to deposit varying percentages of their deposits in an interest-free account with the Bank of Greece as a supplementary means of influencing the total volume of credit. Until 1956, the commercial banks were required to deposit 12 per cent of their private deposits, as well as a certain proportion of the funds deposited with them by public entities. After 1956, this obligation was restricted to private deposits only, and the relevant percentage was reduced to 8 per cent. Since October 1963, the banks have the option of investing 3 per cent of their sight and savings deposits in interest-bearing treasury bills, the percentage of interest-free deposits with the Bank of Greece being correspondingly reduced to 5 per cent. This step taken, among others, with the aim of relaxing credit restrictions, also helped to reduce the burden imposed on the commercial banks by their obligation to maintain noninterest-bearing deposits with the Bank of Greece.

Since December 1957, compulsory deposits have also been used to deal with seasonal variations in commercial bank liquidity. Thus, in December, January, and February, commercial banks are required to deposit a fixed percentage of their sight and savings deposits in an interest-bearing account with the Bank of Greece. Table 24 shows the percentages fixed since 1957 for this purpose.

TABLE 24

Compulsory seasonal deposits of commercial banks with the Bank of Greece
(in percentage terms)

	December	January	February
1957	10	—	—
1958	10	12	14
1959	10	12	14
1960	10	12	14
1961	4	10–12	12
1962	4	6	8
1963	4	6	8
1964	—	8	10

Source: Bank of Greece.

Compulsory commercial bank deposits with the central bank were introduced in order to absorb a part of the commercial banks' increased availabilities as a result of seasonal liquidation of credit extended to the tobacco trade. Before 1957, these availabilities were automatically absorbed, as the tobacco trade was largely financed by Bank of Greece funds. When the commercial banks reduced to a minimum their dependence on central bank credit, this automatic adjustment ceased to operate and increased liquidity led to excessive credit expansion by commercial banks, which the Bank of Greece was obliged to control.

Rediscount of commercial bank portfolio—In the years under review, the credit extended by the Bank of Greece to the commercial banks could not play the role it fulfills under normal conditions, i.e., with the discount rate mechanism

75

in operation. During the phase of stricter quantitative restrictions, the financing of commercial banks with central bank funds was merely an auxiliary means for regulating the volume of credit. In fact, although up to 1955 commercial banks were still largely dependent on central bank credit—extended to them through the participation of the Bank of Greece in their financing of export trade especially tobacco, handicrafts, and to some extent industry—the role of central bank action in determining the total volume of credit was rather limited, as credits to the economy were subject to ceilings fixed by the Currency Committee. When, subsequently, savings accumulated in commercial banks and developed into a major source of funds for financing the economy, the share of Bank of Greece funds in total credit extended by the commercial banks fell from 23.8 per cent in 1953 to 4 per cent in 1957 and has remained ever since almost invariably at the same low level. This has reduced to a minimum the possibility of Bank of Greece control over the total volume of credit through loans to the commercial banks.

Since 1956, commercial banks have been allowed to rediscount their portfolio of industrial bills within limits fixed by the Bank of Greece. Rediscounting and temporary overdraft facilities with the Bank of Greece were adopted to counter temporary shortages of funds in the banking system which might hinder the regular financing of the economy. The mechanism functioned effectively during periods of international crises when deposits were run down, as well as in other periods of temporary shortages.

Compulsory investment in treasury bills—The obligation of the commercial banks to invest a fixed percentage of their sight and savings deposits in treasury bills was an important step taken during the period under review. Although it was also used as a means of exercizing quantitative control over credit, the main aim was to secure funds to finance productive activities under the Government Investment Program. This measure was adopted when the inflow of deposits into the commercial banks started increasing at a faster rate than the demand of firms for short and longer-term capital. Initially, (in 1958), compulsory investment in treasury bills was fixed at 5 per cent of each bank's total sight and savings deposits. This was raised to 10 per cent in 1959 and to 18 per cent in 1961. In 1963, the rate was further raised to 20 per cent, of which at least 2 per cent must be invested in government bonds issued to finance economic development projects.

Public entity funds and Postal Savings Bank deposits—During the period under review, the total volume of credit was also influenced through the control of public entity funds deposited with the commercial banks and through redeposits of funds accumulated in the Postal Savings Bank.

A law, passed in 1950, established the compulsory deposit of public entity and Social Insurance Organization funds with the Bank of Greece and determined the utilization of these funds on the basis of Currency Committee decisions. In conformance with this law, all such deposits with commercial banks in 1950 were transferred in 1951 to the Bank of Greece. The latter redeposited them with the same banks, to be used for the purpose of financing activities previously financed with central bank funds. In 1956, the total amount of these deposits was transferred to the National Bank of Greece, which handled most of the credit extended to particularly favored sectors of the economy, i.e., the export and tobacco trade. Redepositing was subsequently suspended, except for a few isolated cases relating to the finance of specific projects.

Since 1956, Postal Savings Bank funds have been deposited with the commercial banks in order to increase their liquidity. Up to 1959, these deposits rose steadily (from 163 million drachmas in 1956 to 1,139 million drachmas in 1959), while in the following two years, 1960 and 1961, they remained unchanged and began to rise again in 1962 (1,376 million drachmas) and 1963 (1,862 million drachmas).

Selective credit controls

Selective controls—under a stricter form in the early years of the period and relaxed thereafter—have been the main policy instrument in determining both the total volume of credit and its distribution between the sectors of the economy.

Selective credit controls are widely used even in industrial countries with a highly developed money market. It is not unusual in these countries for the authorities to determine credit ceilings or a fixed rate of increase in the credit extended to some branches of economic activity. Recourse to selective controls is considered all the more advisable in countries seeking to develop their economies, where it is imperative to make a stricter evaluation of credit needs. In such countries, if the distribution of credit is left prematurely and exclusively to the commercial banks, it will usually result in a considerable leakage of credit towards activities that are less socially productive, but highly profitable. As credit policy is one of the main instruments for influencing private economic activity, its aim should be to ensure the best possible utilization of scarce resources. Selective controls are, therefore, needed in order to restrict or exclude activities which have a minor or retarding effect on economic development.

During the period under review, the Greek authorities sought to adjust credit to the requirements of economic development and monetary equilibrium by implementing an over-all program which determined credit ceilings by sector of activity. As deposits accumulated in the banks, credit ceilings were raised. Finally, they were applied only to the financing of activities whose expansion beyond certain limits was considered undesirable.

78

In conjunction with quantitative restrictions, the Currency Committee exercized credit control by determining the terms and conditions under which particular transactions could be financed. Preventive control, which was previously applied in the form of Currency Committee approvals for specific cases of financing, was gradually reduced and has become almost completely inoperative since 1957.

A more detailed analysis of the credit policy applied and its effect on the various sectors of economic activity is given in the following paragraphs.

Industry—Preventive control of short-term industrial credit, very strict until 1952, started to be relaxed after that year. Until 1952 all credit, with the exception of discounting three-month commercial bills and financing of raw material imports, was subject to prior approval by the Currency Committee. Preventive credit control was progressively reduced from 1954 onwards and almost completely eliminated in 1957, when full responsibility for specific cases of financing was transferred to the banks. Experience had shown that the constraint of prior approval of credit was ineffective in practice, in so far as the prevention of credit leakage in undesirable directions was concerned. It was, therefore, considered advisable to abolish preventive control by the monetary authorities—said to hinder banks in their operations—and to try out the system of checking the utilization of credit through the banks, on the assumption that they were in a better position to control the firms they financed. However, the expansion of credit to industry in 1957 and 1958 by over four times the rate of increase of industrial production (see Table 25 below), showed that the commercial banks had not succeeded in their new role and were unable to prevent the extensive leakage of credit towards purposes wholly unrelated to industrial activity. The rise in credit at such a rapid rate could not possibly be attributed solely to the substitution of bank credit for

79

loans from sources outside the banking system, however extensive such borrowing may have been in periods when the shortage of funds was greater. Although there must have been a considerable degree of substitution in 1957, the over-all rise in credit during that year and—even less—the increase observed in 1958 cannot be attributed to such a substitution. Another indication of substantial credit leakage is given by the ratio of commercial bill discounts to the total financing of industry for working capital which decreased from 36 per cent in 1955 to 17 per cent in 1958.

TABLE 25

Industrial credit and production

| Year | Short term credits to industry and mining (end of year levels in millions drs) | | | Percentage increases in: | |
	Total	Discounted bills	Working capital	Industrial credit for working capital (average levels)	Industrial production
1954	2,172.0	764.7	1,407.3	31.3	24.0
1955	2,299.8	839.4	1,460.4	17.2	3.2
1956	2,888.3	963.8	1,924.5	11.2	1.3
1957	4,445.8	969.4	3,476.4	41.0	8.0
1958	5,519.9	946.4	4,573.5	43.3	10.0
1959	5,653.2	1,869.0	3,784.2	7.0	1.0
1960	6,595.5	1,944.5	4,651.0	10.5	7.7
1961	7,492.6	2,087.3	5,405.3	18.0	6.2
1962	8,745.8	2,186.2	6,559.6	13.8	5.0
1963	10,249.4	2,414.2	7,835.2	17.6	7.4

Sources: Bank of Greece, National Statistical Service of Greece.

The increase in industrial credit has obviously facilitated the financing of activities which do not contribute to economic development. Credit leakage took place mainly in the direction of financing imports of consumer goods and expanding sales on installment credit, thus assisting an excessive increase in consumption.

The relative inability of commercial banks to secure a more rational distribution of credit according to the aims of economic policy made it necessary to readjust credit policy on a new basis. Thus, at the end of 1958, the Currency Committee introduced a series of general rules to which the commercial banks should conform when extending credit to industry. These rules established a closer relationship between the credit extended to enterprises and their productive activities, and reduced the possibility of credit leakages.

In the subsequent years (1959–1963), while credit expansion continued, the difference between the rate of increase in credit (at average annual levels) and the rate of growth in industrial output was far less than in 1957–1958 (see Table 25). The fact, however, that credit increased at a faster rate than production shows that there is no justification for the view that credit policy was unduly restrictive. Since October 1963, the authorities have lifted all restrictions on credit to industry for working capital by expanding overdraft facilities, the amount of which is no longer linked to a percentage of total annual sales.

Handicraft industry—The credit policy adopted for the handicraft sector was different from that applied to industry and ensured a more favorable treatment for handicraft firms, which continued to receive financing from Bank of Greece funds at a lower (subsidized) interest rate. Up to 1959, loans extended to this sector were subject to prior approval by the Handicrafts Credit Committee. Since then, loans have been granted on the responsibility of the commercial banks. Apart from these low-interest loans, the handicraft enterprises were given credit on the basis of commercial bills and other loans under terms and conditions determined by the Currency Committee. By a series of decisions taken

81

between 1956 and 1963, the credit ceiling for handicraft firms was raised considerably. However, as in the case of industry, the expansion of credit to the handicraft sector after restrictions were lifted was disproportionate to the increase in handicraft production, a fact which is indicative of extensive credit leakage towards other purposes. Since October 1963, all restrictions on credit to handicraft firms for working capital were lifted. Instead, it was stipulated that such credit would be extended on the basis of rules and methods applying to industrial firms.

TABLE 26

Credit to the handicraft sector

End of year	Outstanding balances (in millions drachmas)	Percentage change
1955	123	+ 71
1956	263	+114
1957	426	+ 62
1958	594	+ 40
1959	779	+ 31
1960	1,256	+ 61
1961	1,226	— 2
1962	1,345	+ 10
1963	1,782	+ 33

Source: Bank of Greece.

Export trade — The policy pursued in financing the export trade in general, and tobacco trade in particular, extended highly favorable treatment to these activities, owing to their great importance in the national economy. Up to 1956, the Bank of Greece was involved in two ways in credits granted to these sectors: (1) the Bank provided directly to a large extent for the needs of both the export and tobacco trade; (2) Bank of Greece funds covered 50 per cent of the credit extended by the commercial banks. After

1956, the latter method was replaced by the system of "special loans." Under this system, the commercial banks were obliged to make available 33 per cent of their total deposits for the financing of the export and tobacco trades and a number of other sectors (credit to handicraft firms, short-term industrial credit, etc.). If these funds were not sufficient to satisfy the credit needs of these sectors, the commercial banks were able to use advances from the Bank of Greece. The system of special loans was abolished in 1957, when the availabilities of the commercial banks increased to an extent which made it possible to satisfy all applications for loans under prevailing regulations.

Quantitative restrictions on credit to the export trade were lifted completely in 1959 and commercial banks were empowered to extend credit up to 100 per cent of the value of exported goods for a maximum period of nine months.

Domestic and import trade—Throughout the period under review, credits to domestic and import trade were controlled through quantitative restrictions and credit ceilings fixed for each bank, in order to prevent an excessive expansion of consumer credit and of imports of consumer goods. The specific conditions and terms of financing were determined by the Currency Committee. However, between 1956 and 1963 credit ceilings have been continuously raised at a much faster rate than the increase in turnover of domestic and import trade and the extension of credit to trade has been steadily liberalized.

Interest rate policy—During the major part of the period under review, conditions in the money and capital markets precluded a credit policy which would allow the interest rate to play a free role in the determination of the total volume of credit.

Throughout the period, the main objective of interest rate policy was to reduce the burden of interest on production costs within the limits set by the level of the banks' operating costs which, in turn, was affected to a certain extent by interest rates on deposits. Thus, the pursuit of a policy which would bring deposit rates to lower levels was a condition not only for a general reduction in the cost of borrowing but also for further selective interest rate adjustments according to the needs and importance of each economic sector in the development process.

TABLE 27

Credit ceilings in the finance of domestic trade

End of period	Million drachmas	
1950 Dec.	564	Including discounting of bills and advances on industrial bills of lading.
1951 »	535	
1952 »	615[a]	Including advances on industrial bills of lading, but excluding discounting of industrial bills.
1953 »	411	
1954 »	461	
1955 »	527	
1956 »	661	
1957 »	762	
1958 »	762	
1959 »	1,110	
1960 »	1,190	Credit to industrialists is excluded.
1961 »	1,320	
1962 »	1,320	
1963 Jan.	1,900	
1963 Dec.	2,320	
1964 March	2,550	

a Including credit to the import trade
Source: Bank of Greece.

In the first part of the period, the high cost of banking and consequently the high rate of interest on loans, were mainly due to the limited extent of the banks' lending operations and the resulting large disparity between their earnings and their operating expenses. But even after bank turnover increased, the interest rates on loans had to be maintained at high levels owing to the rise of interest

MONETARY AND CREDIT POLICY
TABLE 28

Interest rates on loans

Date of change	Bank of Greece re-discount rate	To industry Short term	Long term	To handicrafts On special termsa	Other	To export and tobac-co trades	To domes-tic & im-port trades
1950 Jul.	5b	12	12	6–8	12	8	12
1954 Jan.	5b	10	10	6–8	10	8	10
1955 Jan.	5b	9	9	6–8	9	9	9
1956 May	11	10	10	6–8	10	9	10
1956 Aug.	11	10	10	6–8	10	9	10
1956 Nov.	11	10	10	7–9	10	9	10
1957 Mar.	11	10	10	7–9	10	9	10
1959 Apr.	10	9	9	6.5–8	9	8	10
1959 Jul.	10	9	9	5.5–7	9	7	10
1959 Oct.	9	8	7	5.5–7	8	6.5	10
1960 Apr.	7	8	7	5.5–7	7.5	6	10
1960 Nov.	6	8	7	5.5–7	7.5	6	10
1961 Mar.	6	8	7	5.5–7	7.5	6	10
1962 Jan.	6	8c	7c	5.5–7	7.5	6	10
1963 Apr.	5.5	7.5c d	7c	5.5–7	7.5	5.5	8.5f
1963 Oct.	5.5	7.5c d	7c	—	7.5e	5.5	7.5f

General Remarks :

Since Dec. lst, 1959 the interest plus commission on loans from E.D.F.O. funds ranges between 5 and 7 per cent, depending on the individual case. Interest rates in the above table do not include commission (1 to 2 per cent since January 1954 and 1 per cent since October 1963).

a Loans for the purchase of raw materials and equipment renewal

b These rates are of no significance since rediscounting was not practiced before 1956

c In 1962 the rate of interest on loans to export industries was fixed at 4 to 5 per cent plus 1 per cent commission

d For the discounting of bills. Higher rates, up to 9 per cent, are in effect for other forms of short-term financing

e The interest rate is 6.5 per cent on credit to handicraft firms not exceeding 100,000 drachmas

f For the purchase of domestic industrial products. Such finance represents a very small part of total credit

Source: Bank of Greece.

rates on deposits effected in May 1956 in order to attract savings to the banking system. A policy bringing into effect reduced and discriminatory rates of interest on loans was introduced for the first time in 1959, after rates on deposits had again been lowered. By 1962 the pattern of interest rates stood at a substantially lower level than before the new policy.

Direct credit by the Bank of Greece—During the period under review, the Bank of Greece extended direct credit to various sectors of the economy. This practice was gradually discontinued as normal conditions were restored in the money market, and central bank credit was ultimately restricted to the absolute minimum required to ensure reasonable terms of financing in certain special cases.

TABLE 29

Bank of Greece advances in relation to total credit

	Bank of Greece loans to trade and industry as a percentage of total credit extended to these sectors	Bank of Greece direct loans to the private sector as a percentage of total credit extended to this sector [a]
1953	17.3	7.3
1955	12.0	7.8
1958	7.0	4.2
1960	4.0	2.6
1961	3.9	2.5
1962	3.6	3.4
1963	3.7	3.5

[a] Exclusive of loans to the Public Power Corporation, the Autonomous Currants Organization, and the Cooperative Sultana Association
Source: Bank of Greece.

Special problems of agricultural credit

In general, and particularly in developing countries, the extension of credit to the agricultural sector is a special

86

problem which cannot be solved by using the criteria normally employed when the financing of other sectors of economic activity is under consideration. In addition to the general principle that credit policy in a developing country should be adjusted to the requirements of development policy, agricultural credit involves a number of other important criteria. First, when allocating total credit among the various sectors of the economy, it should not be overlooked that the need of the agricultural sector for funds is almost entirely satisfied through bank credit. Second, the terms on which credit is extended to farmers are not determined solely by the importance of agriculture to the national economy. Social and political considerations make it necessary to grant more favorable terms, such as low interest rates, longer periods for repayment, and other facilities.

In Greece, the agricultural sector was financed largely with Bank of Greece funds and constituted one of the major expansionary factors in the money supply. The Agricultural Bank of Greece, despite its extensive network of branch offices, did not increase its deposits to any significant degree. Table 30 shows the development of Agricultural Bank deposits in relation to total liabilities.

TABLE 30

Ratio of deposits to total liabilities of the Agricultural Bank

Years	Deposits as a percentage of total liabilities
1956	7.3
1958	7.2
1960	10.5
1962	13.0
1963	13.5

Source: Bank of Greece.

In view of the inadequacy of the funds at the disposal of the Agricultural Bank, efforts were made to supplement

TABLE 31

Sources of funds of the Agricultural Bank of Greece

Sources	1956 Million drs.	Per cent	1957 Million drs.	Per cent	1958 Million drs.	Per cent	1959 Million drs.	Per cent	1960 Million drs.	Per cent	1961 Million drs.	Per cent	1962 Million drs.	Per cent	1963 Million drs.	Per cent
Public entity funds through Bank of Greece	—		80	(1)	378	(5)	594	(8)	333	(4)	1,090	(11)	1,219	(12)	1,193	(11)
Government funds	413	(9)	467	(8)	476	(7)	722	(9)	800	(9)	651	(7)	541	(5)	469	(4)
Postal Savings Bank deposits	—		—		—		121	(1)	230	(3)	206	(2)	267	(3)	260	(2)
E.D.F.O. deposits	68	(1)	74	(1)	158	(3)	123	(2)	83	(1)	50	—	31	—	2	—
Commercial bank deposits	—		—		—		—		400	(5)	300	(3)	—		—	
U.S. aid funds	—		—		—		—		—		—		400	(4)	800	(7)
Agricultural Bank own funds	823	(17)	919	(16)	993	(14)	1,520	(19)	1,751	(20)	1,983	(21)	2,587	(27)	2,769	(25)
Funds of the Bank of Greece	3,408	(73)	4,298	(74)	4,913	(71)	4,816	(61)	4,969	(58)	5,322	(56)	4,822	(49)	5,767	(51)
Total	4,712	100	5,838	100	6,918	100	7,896	100	8,566	100	9,602	100	9,867	100	11,260	100

Source: Bank of Greece.

88

TABLE 32

Interest rates on credit to agriculture

Date of change	Cultivation loans			Collateral loans			Medium & long-term loans			
	Individual farmers	Cooperatives	Cooperative unions	Individual farmers	Cooperatives	Cooperative unions	Individual farmers	Cooperatives	Cooperative unions	Interest rates on delayed repayments
1949 — Jan.	9	8	7	10.5	9.5	8.5	9.5	8.5	7.5	12
1954 — Jan.	7	6.5	6	8.5	7.5	7	7	6.25	6	12
1957 — Mar.	7	6.5	6	8.5	7.5	7	8	7.25	7	12
1961 — Mar.	6.5	5.75	5.5	7	6.25	6	7	6.25	6	9
1964 — Jan.	5	4.25	4	6	5.25	5	4	3.5	3.5	7

Source: Bank of Greece.

its financial resources by means other than Bank of Greece credit. Public entity funds deposited with the Bank of Greece were used to this end, as well as Postal Savings Bank funds deposited with commercial banks, and government funds. Nonetheless, it was still necessary to continue to assist the Agricultural Bank with Bank of Greece funds, although to a considerably lesser extent than previously.

A parallel effort was made to improve credit terms by reducing interest rates on agricultural loans. The agricultural credit policy pursued between 1956 and 1963 aimed at a continuous increase in credit and especially in medium and long-term loans.

TABLE 33

Outstanding credit to the agricultural sector
(in millions drachmas)

End of year	Total	Cultivation loans	Collateral loans	Other	Long-term loans	Agricultur-al supplies a
1953	2,546.7	1,018.0	701.7	84.9	361.1	381.0
1954	3,229.1	1,337.4	775.2	89.6	376.6	650.3
1955	3,749.1	1,562.9	966.3	90.2	435.3	694.4
1956	4,494.8	1,877.6	1,305.5	168.6	583.1	560.0
1957	5,602.0	2,139.6	1,633.6	222.9	844.6	761.3
1958	6,557.4	2,567.6	1,777.2	224.6	1,307.3	680.7
1959	7,636.5	2,866.1	1,637.7	229.8	1,937.5	965.4
1960	8,193.9	3,113.4	1,585.5	238.9	2,514.9	740.9
1961	9,271.9	3,269.0	2,109.8	242.2	3,061.6	588.4
1962	9,940.9	3,076.1	2,778.6	216.3	3,168.1	701.8
1963	10,761.8	3,750.6	2,684.7	240.5	3,419.8	666.2

a Amounts paid by the Agricultural Bank for the purchase of fertilizers and other supplies
Source: Bank of Greece.

Long-term loans have been increasing at a fast rate and have been rising to an ever-larger proportion of total credit to agriculture, in contrast to the decreasing share of cultivation loans, a fact which in part reflects the gradual reduction of farming costs, as a result of improvements in equipment.

TABLE 34

Outstanding credit to the agricultural sector
(Percentage breakdown)

Year	Total	Cultivation loans	Collateral loans	Other	Long-term loans	Agricultural supplies[a]
1953	100	40.0	27.5	3.3	14.2	15.0
1954	100	41.4	24.0	2.8	11.7	20.1
1955	100	41.7	25.8	2.4	11.6	18.5
1956	100	41.8	29.0	3.7	13.0	12.5
1957	100	38.2	29.2	4.0	15.1	13.5
1958	100	39.1	27.1	3.4	20.0	10.4
1959	100	37.5	21.4	3.0	25.5	12.6
1960	100	38.0	19.3	2.9	30.7	9.1
1961	100	35.3	22.7	2.6	33.0	6.4
1962	100	30.9	27.9	2.2	31.9	7.1
1963	100	34.8	24.9	2.2	31.8	6.3

[a] See note to Table 33
Source: Bank of Greece.

Medium and long-term loans, scheduled on a steadily expanding basis, included to a considerable extent loans bearing a 2 per cent interest rate. However, as shown in Table 33, the total amount actually granted in medium and long-term loans has been declining in recent years, a trend which reflects the limited capacity of the agricultural sector to absorb such loans. This is further verified by comparing low-interest scheduled loans with the amount of loans actually granted. Credit policy is thus shown to have been far from restrictive in the agricultural sector, as is also the case for all the other productive sectors of the economy.

91

TABLE 35

Medium and long-term loans extended by the Agricultural Bank, by source
(loans within each year, in millions drachmas)

Source of credit	1955	1956	1957	1958	1959	1960	1961	1962	1963
Bank of Greece funds (issue money and public entity funds)	61	71	268	411	409	256	1,007	106	279
Government funds	54	171	101	108	374	139	—	—	—
Postal Savings Bank funds	—	—	—	—	139	232	—	163	93
E.D.F.O. funds	45	32	38	101	—	—	—	—	—
Commercial bank funds	—	—	—	—	—	400	—	—	—
U.S. aid counterpart funds	—	—	—	—	—	—	—	400	400
Agricultural Bank's own funds	—	—	90	99	92	88	98	132	192
Other availabilities	—	52	24	19	—	—	—	—	—
Total	160	326	521	738	1,014	1,115	1,105	801	964

Source: Bank of Greece.

Special problems of long-term finance

At the beginning of the period under review, the capital market was practically nonexistent. On the other hand, it was virtually impossible for commercial banks to finance investment while private savings were not accumulating in the banking system.

The measures taken with a view to tackling this problem effectively and to the extent necessary to accelerate economic development, sought to achieve two objectives. First, to take advantage of every existing opportunity to accumulate funds and channel them towards top priority investment through the banking system and other specialized credit organizations. Second, to facilitate the gradual development of the capital market by creating or reforming institutions which could contribute to this end and by introducing incentives which could make investment in securities attractive to the public.

In subsequent years, long-term finance was provided by the Economic Development Financing Organization (E.D.F.O.), which succeeded the Central Loans Committee in 1954, and by the commercial banks. E.D.F.O. resources were provided by U.S. counterpart funds.

The funds for long-term loans granted by the commercial banks derived from public entity funds deposited with the commercial banks, deposits accumulated by the Postal Savings Bank, and private savings deposits with the commercial banks. Although in Greece savings deposits can be immediately withdrawn, in practice the bulk of them have a low turnover and, consequently, it was not considered unsafe to utilize them for long-term loans. Moreover, the climate of confidence in the national currency has substantially lessened the likelihood of a fall-off in public willingness to deposit funds with the banks.

In order to mobilize savings deposits for the financing of investment, the commercial banks have been required since 1957 to utilize 10 per cent (raised subsequently to 15 per cent) of their total deposits for medium and long-term loans, mainly to industrial firms. It has also been stipulated that if these amounts are not used for the required purpose, they should be deposited in a special interest-bearing account with the Bank of Greece, from which they can be drawn only for the purpose outlined above. Loans in this category were initially required to have the prior approval of the Subcommittee on Credit, but since 1960 they have been entrusted to the discretion of the commercial banks. This practice of earmarking 15 per cent of commercial bank deposits for medium and long-term loans played a basic role in placing

PROBLEMS AND METHODS

credit on a sound basis by clearing up the dangerous situation created by large-scale "freezing" of short-term credit.

TABLE 36

Interest rates on long-term credit

Date of change	Interest rates
1954 Jan.	10
1955 Jan.	9
1956 May	10
1959 April	9
1959 Oct.	7

Source: Bank of Greece.

In conjunction with an improvement in the availability of long-term credit, the authorities also sought to introduce favorable terms on loans. The interest rates on long-term loans were lowered and in a large number of cases the Greek economy presents the unusual phenomenon of rates on long-term lending lower than those on short-term credit.

The preceding analysis shows that credit policy during the period under review was to a high degree efficiently adapted to satisfy the credit requirements of economic development. The phenomenon of the limited demand for funds to realize productive investment, particularly in view of the great need for growth-promoting investment activity, supports our basic hypothesis which applies to most developing economies—namely that the major obstacle to rapid growth is the lack of entrepreneurial initiative, organizing ability, and a skilled labor force.

94

III

FISCAL POLICY

INTRODUCTION

Fiscal policy in a less-developed country can make an important contribution towards achieving the parallel and complementary objectives of economic development and monetary stability. Due regard must, however, be given to a more equitable distribution of income, which should be a basic goal of social policy. This is essential to the success of development policy because it provides a powerful incentive for the population to participate wholeheartedly in the growth effort.

The principal objectives of fiscal policy, which are of basic importance both to monetary stability and the pace of the development process are : First, a balanced ordinary budget[1] and the creation of possibilities for surpluses on current account which would be a source of finance for the investment budget. Second, a substantial improvement in the structure of government expenditure to enable the rapid and effective creation of the necessary infrastructure, with high priority given to key sectors such as education and organization. Although these two basic objectives of fiscal policy are directly interdependent, the importance of economic infrastructure has mainly been stressed as a precondition for development, whereas the need to achieve a balance in the current budget has chiefly been regarded as an essential

---

[1] The terms *ordinary* and *current budget* are used interchangeably in the text. The current budget includes the ordinary revenue and expenses of the Administration. The investment budget or program refers to expenditure for gross capital formation and revenue therefrom. The consumer goods account consists mainly of expenses and receipts originating from policies of price and income support for the agricultural sector.

prerequisite for monetary stability. It is evident, however, that both objectives contribute simultaneously to economic development and monetary stability.

Public expenditure

The excessive expansion of current public expenditures and the resulting budgetary deficit have been the principal factors which have upset monetary equilibrium in many developing economies. It should also be emphasized that monetary policy is largely powerless in face of the inflationary pressures created by mismanagement in the fiscal sector.

The structure of public expenditure is an important factor in determining the pace of economic development. It is essential to the effective economic progress of a country to have an adequate infrastructure, and the latter must inevitably be provided by the public sector. The provision of services of strategic importance to economic development, such as education, in particular technical and professional training, also depends on the level of public investment devoted to this end. Furthermore, the relative inadequacy of private initiative makes it necessary for the state to participate in investment activities over a wide area of the economy. The financing of these expenditures calls for a curb on the consumption spending of the public sector. Inflationary pressures generated by deficit consumption spending in the public sector inevitably lead to restrictive policies in other sectors, for instance the financing of private activity. Such restrictions, while necessary for maintaining monetary stability hamper the development of the economy, inasmuch as a larger proportion of total expenditure is devoted to public consumption at the expense of public and private investment. A check on public consumption spending is not, however, an easy task, especially in cases where a large part of it is devoted to defense. External assistance thus provides the only way out of the dilemma created by the need for a high rate of development and the requirements of national and supranational security.

The aims and methods of fiscal policy in an under-developed economy differ substantially from those in a developed country. In terms of general objectives, functional finance in a developed economy has been used mainly to stabilize aggregate consumption and investment demand at a level which ensures full employment with the minimum degree of inflation. The role of fiscal policy in a developing country is different. The principal aim here is to enlarge the productive capacity of the economy by increasing aggregate saving and investment and ensuring a more efficient allocation of resources. The need to promote the development effort imposes on fiscal policy the task, not only of exerting a general influence on aggregate demand and supply, but also of effecting structural readjustments in the economy. While the maintenance of monetary equilibrium requires that effective demand be adjusted to the corresponding level of aggregate supply, economic development also depends on the distribution of available resources between consumption and saving-investment and is determined by the structure of the latter.

Inasmuch as the principles of "functional" fiscal policy have their origin in the interwar depression experienced by advanced economies, they cannot usefully be applied to developing economies. Experience has shown that the structural underemployment and low-income level of the less-developed economies are little, if at all, improved by deficit-financed increases in public consumption spending, while the latter constitute an effective antidote to economic depression in advanced economies. Whereas in the early postwar years there was a tendency to attempt parallels, it has now been generally acknowledged that there are crucial differences between the problems of developing countries and those of advanced economies in a state of

97

depression. Since the central problem for developing economies refers to the relative inadequacy of savings and their use for nonproductive purposes, the role of fiscal policy assumes a different perspective. In developing economies savings are of strategic importance for the financing of the growth process. Therefore, economic development requires the pursuit of a fiscal policy which will ensure that savings are augmented and allocated to the most productive effect. An effective system of tax incentives must be devised and, if necessary, there should be an expansion of the economic activities of the public sector. Such an expansion, however, is not always a satisfactory solution, not only because it may run counter to the institutional framework of a free enterprise economy, but principally because the public sector in an underdeveloped economy suffers from weaknesses similar to those of private enterprise.

Tax incentives

Policy-makers in developing economies are faced with the dilemma of choosing between the revenue aspect of fiscal measures and the creation of effective development incentives. The yields from higher tax rates are often negligible and may sometimes become negative, as a result of the adverse influence of a heavy tax burden on private productive activity. This depends, of course, on a variety of factors such as the structure of the tax system, per capita income, income distribution, the pattern of the economy, the ability of private business to take growth-promoting initiatives, etc. Generally speaking, it may be argued that the adverse effect of a heavy tax burden on production incentives is stronger in less-advanced economies, where entrepreneurship is qualitatively and quantitatively inadequate. Also, an unduly heavy tax burden prevents the lower income groups from enjoying the advantages of economic development and thus discourages them from taking an active part in the necessary efforts. The question of levying heavy taxes on the non-

98

productive accumulation of wealth and land property, on speculative activities, and the consumption of luxuries involves wholly different considerations.

The optimum size of tax revenue depends on the economy's taxable capacity and the effectiveness of the tax-collecting system. It is generally true that in less-developed economies the taxable capacity is not adequately exploited. For a satisfactory assessment of the tax base it is not enough merely to enact the required legislation; it is also necessary to organize a well functioning tax-collection service of unquestionable integrity. To the extent that the latter condition remains only partly fulfilled in a number of under-developed countries, the introduction of higher tax rates might create a strong incentive for tax evasion. (Insofar as the practice of tax evasion involves some degree of risk and considerable organizational expenses, it will naturally vary in intensity according to the benefit derived from the evasion of tax). Moreover, the structure of developing economies and the size of productive units are generally of such a nature that the socioeconomic and administrative costs involved in assessing the tax base justify large-scale tax exemption. It should also be stressed that sociopolitical considerations impose considerable restrictions on tax policy, which cannot always be justified on purely economic grounds.

It is important, therefore, that advanced economies which provide development funds should recognize that the margins for increasing tax revenue in the developing econo-mies are narrow in the short run. Improvements in tax legislation and especially in the tax assessment and collection service require prolonged efforts that cannot be forced to yield impressive results within a relatively short period of time.

FISCAL POLICY DURING THE PERIOD 1950–1963

Introduction

During the period under review, fiscal policy in Greece was faced with an extremely difficult task, inasmuch as its aim was not merely to stimulate economic development without disruptive effects on monetary equilibrium, but to eliminate the widespread inflationary influence of the current budget so as to create the necessary conditions for a sustained increase in the rate of economic development.

As long as the ordinary budget continued to show large deficits, it was impossible to pursue a fiscal policy that would serve the objectives of economic development. Current budget deficits led to continuous increases in currency circulation. Although monetary policy could to a certain extent control the inflationary pressures resulting from other sources, it was basically unable to check the inflationary pressures generated by budgetary deficits. These pressures made it necessary to adopt restrictive policies towards other sectors (e.g., the financing of the private sector). This practice, necessary to maintain monetary equilibrium, exercized a restraining influence on the development of the economy as it entailed the restriction of private expenditure on investment. Thus, a sound budget was a basic condition not only for the restoration of monetary equilibrium but also for the promotion of economic development through fiscal measures.

An indication of the improvement in Greek public finances since 1950 is given by the following comparison. In the fiscal year 1950/51 the ordinary budget, excluding foreign aid granted in order to meet current expenditures, left a deficit of 1,313 million drachmas, while expenditure under the government investment program amounted to 2,349 million drachmas. The ordinary budget for 1963 left a surplus of 1,349 million drachmas and investment expenditure amounted to 5,035 million drachmas.

The aims and objectives of fiscal policy were shaped to meet the major problem faced during each of the two phases of the period under review. In the first phase, i.e., from 1950 to 1956, the ordinary budget was in heavy deficit and therefore, the main problem was to balance the budget.

100

Furthermore, prevailing inflationary conditions made necessary a reduction in the government investment program, as there had been a substantial cut in U.S. aid and the possibility of contracting public consumption expenditure was small. The second phase began after 1956, and was characterized by a surplus in the current budget and the restoration of monetary equilibrium. During this phase it became possible to make effective use of fiscal instruments in promoting the economic development of the country. The basic problems in the fiscal sector during this period were first, to increase the surplus in the current budget by making further efforts to achieve a sound budgetary position and second, to secure the means to finance an extensive government investment program.

During the second phase of the period the authorities made extensive use of fiscal tools in promoting economic development. On the one hand, they sought to control increases in currency circulation that might result in an excessive rise of consumption expenditure. On the other hand, an effort was made to expand investment activity through the budget. To this end, as mentioned in the previous chapter, interest-bearing treasury bills were introduced and have been used extensively since 1958.

The period between 1950 and 1956

Between 1950 and 1956 U.S. aid continued to provide the main outlet for the inflationary pressures originating in the public and private sectors of the economy. It was, however, made available on a far smaller scale than in the years before 1950. This in turn limited the possibility of undertaking public investment and reduced the available margins for financing the private sector. Thus, the level of both these magnitudes came to depend on the success of the effort made to reduce the deficit in the ordinary budget, inasmuch as private savings, besides being inadequate,

101

remained outside the banking system and could not be utilized by economic policy. On the other hand, given the prevailing climate of inflation, an expansion in the currency circulation beyond certain limits would have entailed great risks.

TABLE 37

Ordinary budget deficits and government investment
(in millions drachmas at current prices)

	1950/51	1951/52	1952/53	1953/54	1954/55	1955/56 18 months
Ordinary budget deficits	1,313	749	161	486	644	459
Government investment expenditure	2,439	1,716	1,458	1,275	1,397	1,792

Sources: For ordinary budget deficits, "Provisional Balance Sheets" and "Actual Budgets," 1950/51–1955/56 of the General Accounting Office. Reconstruction expenditures (category IV) covered by special U.S. aid and included in the investment budget have been substracted from ordinary budget expenditures. For public investment expenditures: For fiscal years 1950/51 and 1951/52, U.S.O.M./Greece, *Statistical Data Book 1954/55 and First Half of Fiscal Year 1955/56*, Volume II, February 1956, Table 125. For fiscal years 1952/53–1955/56, General Accounting Office.

The fiscal policy pursued during the period 1951 to 1956 brought about a considerable reduction in the ordinary budget deficit. In 1952/53 the deficit dropped to a very low level, rising again in the next two years as a result of substantial expenditures for the provision of relief to earthquake victims. Successive and substantial reductions during the fiscal years 1951 through 1954 brought the total of public investment expenditure down to approximately half the corresponding magnitude in 1950/51 and the level of public investment remained substantially below that of 1950/51 until the end of 1956.

102

As a result of the substantial reduction in the deficit of the ordinary budget and the maintenance of government investment expenditure at relatively low levels, the annual fiscal deficits were less than, or about equal to, the amount of U.S. aid counterpart funds during the period, except for the 18 months of the fiscal year 1955/56.

TABLE 38

Fiscal deficits and absorption of U.S. aid counterpart funds

(in millions drachmas at current prices)

| Fiscal year | Fiscal deficits | | | U.S. counter-part funds c |
	Budget a	Consumer goods account b	Total	
1950/51	3,311	—241	3,070	3,806
1951/52	2,104	581	2,685	2,890
1952/53	1,252	—342	910	1,796
1953/54	1,332	406	1,738	1,542
1954/55	1,742	— 71	1,725	1,607
1955/56 (18 months)	2,326	948	3,274	2,420

a Aggregate of ordinary and investment budget minus the deficit covered by transfers and loans from abroad (other than U.S. aid), plus the uncovered deficits in the consumer goods accounts

b Bank of Greece advances to cover changes in inventories and in debts or claims (except those referring to management deficits) under the government consumer goods accounts. For 1955/56 the figures include the increase in debit balances in the Agricultural Bank's account for tobacco purchases on behalf of the government and in the special accounts of the Cooperative Sultana Association and the Autonomous Currants Organization

c Excluding the percentage appropriated to cover U.S. government expenses in Greece

Sources: For fiscal deficits, the same as for Table 37. For U.S. counterpart funds, General Accounting Office, *Bulletin of Fiscal Data,* September 1961.

The fact that during this period fiscal deficits were reduced in proportion with the substantial decreases in U.S. aid, made it possible to use the greater part of the rapidly increasing private savings for meeting the capital needs of the private sector and to reduce the inflationary pressures arising from the financing of this sector. Thus, the developments in the fiscal sector described above, also contributed to the restoration of monetary equilibrium.

TABLE 39

Gross national product and private savings at current prices
(in millions drachmas)

Year	Gross national product	Private savings	Private savings as a percentage of G.N.P.
1950	28,837	835	2.9
1951	35,863	1,153	3.2
1952	37,937	940	2.5
1953	50,280	3,037	6.0
1954	58,690	1,934	3.3
1955	66,557	4,443	6.7
1956	77,729	5,607	7.2

Source: Ministry of Coordination, "*National Accounts of Greece, 1948-1959,*" Volume 9, 1961 Tables 2 and 11.

The period between 1957 and 1963

Following the gradual reduction in the ordinary budget deficit during the period, 1957 was marked by a surplus of some 200 million drachmas. Since 1958, the surplus in the ordinary budget (after allowing for the uncovered management deficits in the consumer goods account and subsidies given through it) has risen substantially to an annual average of 920 million drachmas during the period 1958 to 1963. These surpluses—which together with the revenue from investments constituted the contribution of the State to total savings—were used to finance a substantial part of government

TABLE 40

Government investment, fiscal deficits and sources of finance
(in millions drachmas)

	1957	1958	1959	1960	1961	1962	1963[a]
I. ORDINARY BUDGET							
a. Revenue	13,005	13,901	14,297	15,196	17,751	19,515	21,380
b. Expenditure	12,876	12,961	13,971	14,498	16,284	18,092	19,936
c. Balance[b]	+ 129	+ 940	+ 326	+ 698	+1,467	+1,423	+1,444
II. INVESTMENT BUDGET							
a. Revenue	166	221	426	530	592	637	543
b. Expenditure	2,218	2,595	3,374	4,144	5,056	5,850	5,035
c. Balance	−2,052	−2,374	−2,948	−3,614	−4,464	−5,213	−4,492
III. CONSUMER GOODS ACCOUNT[c] Increase (−) or decrease (+) in debit balances	−1,063	− 338	+ 356	− 432	+ 94	−1,067	+ 465
IV. OVER-ALL BALANCES (I + II + III)	−2,986	−1,772	−2,266	−3,348	−2,903	−4,857	−2,583
V. FINANCING							
A. FOREIGN SOURCES	1,561	673	1,027	1,593	1,834	1,453	98
B. DOMESTIC SOURCES	1,425	1,099	1,239	1,755	1,069	3,404	2,485
Bond issues	—	—	2	13	760	996	1,510
Treasury bills	—	545	1,196	995	380	1,084	600
Advances from funds of public entities	289	50	105	—	—	136	450
Bank of Greece advances[d]	1,136	504	−64	747	−71	1,188	−75

[a] Provisional data

[b] Ordinary budget surplus before borrowing and foreign aid, minus uncovered deficit arising from the management of supplies and subsidies of the consumer goods account

[c] (—)denotes an increase in Bank of Greece advances to cover changes in reserves and debts and claims (except those referring to management deficits and subsidies) under the consumer goods account, plus an increase in debit balances in the Agricultural Bank's account for tobacco purchases on behalf of the government and in the special accounts of the Cooperative Sultana Association and the Autonomous Currants Organization. (+) denotes a reduction in these advances and debit balances

[d] Includes the use of treasury availabilities

Sources: For items I, II, IV and V (except for Bank of Greece advances), General Accounting Office. For item III and for Bank of Greece advances, Bank of Greece.

105

investment. This investment increased at a rate ranging from 18 to 30 per cent annually over the 1957–1962 period. Apart from government savings, relatively extensive use was also made of private savings in financing public investment. Foreign sources, which financed about one-third of the total expenditure on investment during the period under review, consisted of about 50 per cent loans and various forms of foreign credit.

Table 40 shows that in order to finance a constantly increasing amount of government investment during the period 1957–1963, the government resorted to domestic borrowing through the issue of bonds and treasury bills and to advances from the Bank of Greece. The latter method was mainly used to cover, on a provisional basis, outlays under the consumer goods account which were the consequence of the government's agricultural price support policy and it had an expansionary effect on the money supply.

Tax policy

Tax policy had two main tasks to perform during the period under review. In the first place, it had to facilitate the restoration of monetary stability of which the prerequisite was a balanced ordinary budget and, in the second place, it had to contribute to economic development by creating government savings and encouraging private savings and investment. At the same time, it was necessary to improve the tax system in such a way as to distribute the tax burden more equitably.

Revenue considerations were of great importance throughout the period under review, but they played a major role in the orientation of tax policy during the years up to 1955/56, when the current budget resulted in a persistent deficit every year. By contrast, social and political considerations and the promotion of economic development were given prominence after 1957 when the current budget finally showed a surplus and monetary equilibrium was firmly established.

Shaping tax policy so as both to safeguard stability and promote economic development is a task which meets with great difficulties. One of the problems to be faced is determining the tax burden on higher incomes—as a rule the main source of savings—at a level which does not adversely affect tax revenue and the propensity to invest. The weaknesses in tax administration make it extremely difficult to control the incidence of the tax burden and restrict the effectiveness of tax policy as a means of influencing the economic behavior of taxpayers.

It has already been mentioned that the main problem of tax policy between 1950 and 1955 was to increase revenue in order to balance the current budget. Efforts were made to improve the procedure of tax assessment and collection and to reorganize the tax collecting services. These efforts were accompanied by several tax adjustments. The increase in revenue achieved as a result was the most important of the period 1950 to 1955 and made a decisive contribution towards balancing the budget. However, these measures resulted in a substantial increase in the tax burden imposed on lower income groups and although many of the new or increased taxes also affected the higher income groups, the over-all effect of these measures on the distribution of the total tax burden was a greater inequality in taxation. Moreover, some of these tax measures brought about an increase in production costs. Nevertheless, by balancing the budget and, possibly, by restraining total consumption expenditures fiscal policy contributed significantly to the restoration of monetary equilibrium.

Although up to 1956 tax policy was oriented mainly towards increasing revenue, various efforts were also made to adjust the tax system according to social and political considerations and to use it as an instrument in promoting economic development. Thus, improvements in the tax system were brought about largely by readjustments made in taxes on income between 1951 and 1954. The first relevant measure was taken in the fiscal year 1951/52 when a progressive tax rate (15 to 35 per cent) was substituted for the proportional rate (36 per cent) previously in effect on income from buildings, land, and securities. Other readjustments were the doubling of income allowances on salaries, the reduction in tax rates on the profits of commercial and industrial firms, and lastly, a decrease in the surtax burden by raising the minimum surtax liability level. These adjustments appear to have rendered the income tax more progressive and to have reduced the tax burden on lower-income groups.

A number of other measures created tax incentives intended to facilitate the country's economic development. Ships of Greek register were made subject to a favorable tax system and newly built ships hoisting the Greek flag enjoyed complete exemption from tax payments over a number of years. Various advantages were also introduced in favor of foreign capital invested in the industrial sector of the Greek economy. These measures included provision for an unchanged tax regime over a period of time for enterprises established with foreign capital, and exemption from customs duties on imported machinery and equipment. Tax facilities were also extended to similar domestic enterprises, of which the output contributed towards saving foreign exchange. An amount scaled up to 10 per cent of annual profits earned by Greek enterprises was tax exempt if used to finance new productive investment or to build up special reserves to expand operations. At the same time, an additional depreciation allowance was granted, up to 2.5 per cent for buildings and 6 per cent for other installations. The exemption from tax of interest earned on bank deposits was extended to cover interest and premiums of the 1954 bond issue. Finally, to promote industrial dispersion and foster regional development, the tax facilities for industrial concerns established outside the area of Attica were improved.

The tax policy applied after 1956 is characterized by a

stronger effort to formulate a more equitable and development-conducive tax system. However, the reforms made in both these directions were of limited effectiveness.

The introduction of a unified progressive income tax in the fiscal year 1955/1956 was the major tax reform of the postwar period. This modernization in the system of direct taxation replaced the outdated and defective schedular system and the surtax on total personal income exceeding a certain amount and it was necessary in order to improve and simplify tax collection, increase the yield of income tax, and render the tax system more equitable. Income-tax reform was carried a step further in 1959 by the extension of the unitary tax system to corporations following which the additional 10 per cent tax levied up to then on undistributed profits was abolished.

An endeavor was also made to pursue a tax policy favorable to economic development by the readjustment of taxes on property and the extension of tax incentives. Thus, in order to stimulate productive investment, the maximum depreciation rates on new installations were raised, the appreciation of assets was exempted from income tax if appropriated to provision for depreciation of installations, and 50 per cent of the net profits of industrial and handicraft firms was tax exempt if spent on new installations. Other specific tax incentives were: the higher percentage of tax exempt net profits, introduced to encourage provincial industries and hotel enterprises; the deduction of an amount corresponding to between 1 and 4 per cent of gross export earnings from the taxable profits of enterprises exporting Greek products, and the tax reductions and exemptions granted to newly established, merging, or expanding firms.

Measures related to tax collection were also taken to offset the reduction in public revenue resulting from the tax reform described above and to restrain the expansionary tendency of consumption, especially in luxuries. In 1958 and in 1960, new consumer taxes were introduced and those

109

already in force were increased to reduce spending on luxury articles.

A comparison between revenue from taxation and national income during the period under review shows that no important change was effected in the relative tax burden. As far as the distribution of the tax burden is concerned, it is worth noting that the share of direct taxes in the national income has somewhat decreased.

TABLE 41

Central government tax revenue as a percentage of national income

	1956	1957	1958	1959	1960	1961	1962	1963[a]
Direct taxes	4.0	4.1	4.2	3.6	3.6	3.8	4.0	3.6
Indirect taxes	11.9	12.4	12.7	12.3	12.7	12.4	12.8	13.3
Total	15.9	16.5	16.9	15.9	16.3	16.2	16.8	16.9

[a] Estimates

Source: Ministry of Coordination, *Greek National Accounts, 1948-1959*, Volume 9, 1961 and *1958-1962*, Volume 12, 1963.

The low ratio of direct taxes is a usual phenomenon in the less-developed countries. It is partly due to income distribution, which is marked by the existence of a very large number of incomes at subsistence level and, therefore, exempt from income tax. This is also observed in Greece, where almost all income from agriculture is exempted from income tax. However, this low ratio in part also reflects a certain degree of tax evasion, commonly found in less developed economies and due mainly to weaknesses in the system of tax collection. In Greece, the relatively high income-tax rates are another reason for tax evasion. In the upper income brackets, the tax rate plus additional charges for the Farmers' Insurance Organization reaches 69 per cent. In consequence, incomes are hit harder than in many large industrial countries with a highly progressive tax burden. This can be seen in Table 42, which compares the tax rates in effect in Greece and those of selected countries, for the same income bracket.

TABLE 42

Percentage of income tax (principal and additional) on earned income in selected countries in 1960

Income level	Belgium	France	West Germany	GREECE a	Italy	Nether-lands	United Kingdom
£ 500	4.8	...	0.3	0.5	5.8	5.2	...
£ 1,000	9.9	3.7	10.9	4.2	9.1	12.7	7.7
£ 1,500	12.5	6.9	14.5	7.7	10.9	19.4	...
£ 2,500	16.5	11.1	21.0	13.6	13.0	29.7	21.9
£ 5,000	26.2	20.4	29.4	30.8	15.6	43.3	35.4
£ 10,000	33.7	29.4	38.2	47.7	18.8	54.9	...
£ 15,000	36.4	34.3	43.2	54.6	21.0	60.0	62.0
Maximum marginal tax rate	43.0	52.8	57.2	69.0	61.2	70.5	88.75
Effective on incomes over £	12,500	16,300	18,900	11,900	315,000	12,200	15,000

a Including charge for Farmers' Insurance Organization

Source: For foreign countries: E.B. Nortcliffe, "Common Market Fiscal Systems" in the series *The British Tax Review Guides*, Number 2, London 1960.

As previously mentioned, the heavier the tax burden, the stronger the incentive for tax evasion which, apart from the risk of subsequent penalties, is also expensive to organize.

Limiting tax evasion is very essential, not only for considerations of greater tax equity but also because tax evasion minimizes the stimulating capacity of tax incentives and thus diminishes the effectiveness of a valuable policy instrument for influencing private economic activity. Indeed, the limited effectiveness of the tax incentives introduced so far is not wholly unrelated to the large extent of tax evasion.

Although it is difficult to assess the effect of the heavier burden from indirect taxes on private consumption, an indication that it may have contributed towards containing expansionary tendencies in private consumption is provided by the fact that the period under review was characterized by a lower average propensity to consume. The decline in average propensity to consume is, of course, also related to the increase in national income which has taken place in recent years.

TABLE 43

Indirect taxes and private consumption as a percentage
of gross national product

	1956	1957	1958	1959	1960	1961	1962	1963a
Indirect taxes	10.1	10.5	10.7	10.4	10.7	10.4	10.6	11.0
Private consumption	77.1	76.2	76.6	74.8	75.2	73.2	72.7	72.1

a Estimates

Source : Ministry of Coordination, *Greek National Accounts 1948–1959*, Vol. 9, 1961 and *1958–1962, Volume 12*, 1963.

Short-term increases in indirect taxes made an important contribution towards achieving monetary stability, and were applied during periods marked by inflationary pressures in the private sector. In 1957 and 1958, for instance, strong expansionary tendencies in consumption—reflected in a substantial rise in imports during 1958—were met by imposing special consumption taxes and raising other taxes, as mentioned above.

The general conclusion to be drawn from the preceding survey is that, although fiscal policy succeeded in obtaining a satisfactory volume of revenue and contributed to the restoration of monetary equilibrium, there was not an equivalent progress towards achieving greater tax equity, effecting the reorganization of the revenue services, and establishing better relations between taxpayers and the State.

There must be a more progressive trend in taxation if a more equitable distribution of income is to be achieved. This objective is of basic importance to economic development and must be a principal aim of fiscal policy. It is essential to reform the fiscal system on the basis of these considerations and it is equally imperative that the revenue services should be better organized to carry out their task to better effect and with greater justice.

It is not enough, however, to ensure an equitable sharing of the tax burden. Taxpayers must be treated in a manner which helps to relieve their uncertainties and overcome their reservation towards the tax authorities. From this point of view, the retroactive taxes imposed at the beginning of the period under review had an unfavorable impact. If taxpayers and enterprises liable to taxation are to carry out their economic projects successfully and to meet their tax obligations willingly and conscientiously, they must operate under an unambiguous and well-defined fiscal regime, with a minimum of surprises to dislocate their plans.

Among the objectives of an improved fiscal system, the elimination of tax evasion holds a prominent place. As already pointed out, the tendency to tax evasion is strengthened by the very high rates of taxation. With this in mind, it might be possible to envisage a certain lowering of rates which, by making tax evasion less attractive, could lead to an increase in total revenue. This would, however, require an efficiently functioning tax administration, and an improvement in the relations between tax authorities and taxpayers.

Current expenditure

During the period under review it was important to maintain

public spending at a level that would minimize the risk of severe inflationary pressures. At the same time it was necessary to change the structure of expenditure in such a way as to serve the aims of economic development. To this end, it was necessary to restrain the expansionary trend of consumption expenditure—particularly forms of consumption, the expansion of which would exercize an adverse influence on economic development—and to increase investment expenditure. Until 1956, the budget deficits incurred every year made it necessary to limit public investment expenditure. From 1957 onwards, the main task of fiscal policy in this connection was to improve the structure of public expenditure in order to make it more productive. During this latter phase, increased public outlays to finance an expanding investment program were hardly limited by the need to preserve monetary equilibrium. In the last few years before 1963, almost the only factor to determine the level of investment expenditure was the absorptive capacity of the economy.

The adjustment of public expenditure policy to satisfy these objectives was made more difficult by the inelasticity of large items of public expenditure and by the technical and organizational inadequacies of the public sector. Deficits incurred in the consumer goods account were another difficult problem. These deficits represent expenditure on subsidies to protect agricultural income through price supports for agricultural products. In addition, the large-scale government purchases of agricultural products resulted in most years in large cash outlays, with expansionary effects on currency circulation.

An adverse influence on the economy was also exercized by government subsidies extended to cover the deficits incurred by the State railways. The monetary authorities made continuous efforts to cut subsidies and, especially, to readjust them so that they would promote instead of retard economic development.

The financing of government investment

The expansion of resources to finance development-promoting public investment was the other side of the fiscal problem during the period under review. In the first period (1950–1956), the reduction of investment expenditure was unavoidable, given the sharp decrease in U.S. aid and the large deficits in the ordinary budget. After 1957, however, investment spending rose at a very high rate. For the period 1957–1963, total investment expenditure—including investment undertaken by the Public Power Corporation, the Greek Telecommunications Organization, the Workers' Housing Organization, and the long-term loans extended by the Agricultural Bank of Greece and the Economic Development Financing Organization—amounted to over four times the corresponding expenditure for the period 1950/51–1955/56.

During the period when the contribution made by U.S. grants in aid dropped to about 13 per cent of total government investment, funds for its further financing were sought in domestic savings and loans from foreign sources. From 1957 to 1963 savings in the form of budget surpluses and revenue from investment covered 34 per cent of government investment expenditure. These savings were supplemented to a considerable degree by drawing on private savings through borrowing while foreign loan funds—mainly foreign government loans and credit for importing capital goods—financed about 15 per cent of total expenditure.

The utilization of private savings through bond issues and treasury bills became possible after the restoration of monetary stability and the provision of certain guarantees to the buyers of securities. The restoration of confidence in the credit-worthiness of the government and other public entities is reflected in the fact that all bond issues so far have been fully subscribed. The issue of treasury bills—which to some extent was an indirect way of drawing from private savings, since the bills were largely bought by commercial

115

TABLE 44

Financing of the government investment program during the period 1950/51—1955/56
(in millions drachmas)

	1950/51	1951/52	1952/53	1953/54	1954/55	1955/56
Investment Expenditure Financing	2,439	1,716	1,458	1,275	1,397	1,792
1. Foreign sources	3,904	2,268	1,045	1,807	1,398	1,700
U.S. aid—Donations	3,463c	1,938d	705c	1,455	1,080	1,184
U.S. aid—Loans	—	—	—	—	240	510
Other foreign loans and credits	—	—	—	151	—	—
Reparations	441	330	340	201	78	6
Other	—	—	—	—	—	—
2. Domestic sources	—1,313	— 718	— 134	— 331	262	— 215
Ordinary budget surplusb	—1,313	— 749	— 233	— 604	— 674	— 799
Revenue from government investment	—	31	99	195	251	259
Bond issues	—	—	—	78	217	—
Treasury bills	—	—	—	—	—	—
Advances from funds of public entities	—	—	—	—	468e	325e
3. Bank of Greece advances and Treasury availabilitiesf	—152	166	547	— 201	— 263	307

(For notes see Table 45)

Sources (for both Tables 44 and 45): General Accounting Office : "Actual Budgets" 1950/51–1959, Bulletin of Fiscal Data August 1961 and General Balance Sheets of the State. Provisional Revenue Records 1959–1963. Data on foreign resources for the fiscal years 1950/51 and 1951/52 : U.S.O.M./Finance and Program Division, *Statistical Data Book 1954/55 and First Half of Fiscal Year 1955/56*, Volume II, February 1956, Table 125.

TABLE 45

Financing of the government investment program during the period 1957—1963
(in millions drachmas)

	1957	1958	1959	1960	1961	1962	1963h
Investment Expenditure Financing	2,218	2,595	3,374	4,144	5,056	5,850	5,035
1. Foreign sources	1,561	673	1,027	1,593	1,834	1,453	98
U.S. aid—Donations	550	326	644	752	663	559	33
U.S. aid—Loans	705	345	331	73	323	138	25
Other foreign loans and credits	303	—	22	737	822	403	—
Reparations	3	2	3	4	7	329	—
Other	—	—	27	27	19	23	40
2. Domestic sources	584	1,756	2,055	2,236	3,199	4,276	4,547
Ordinary budget surplusb	129	940	326	698	1,467	1,423	1,444
Revenue from government investment	166	221	426	530	592	637	543
Bond issues	—	—	2	13	760	996	1,510
Treasury bills	—	545	1,196	995	380	1,084	600
Advances from funds of public entities	289e	50	105g	—	—	136g	450g
3. Bank of Greece advances and Treasury availabilitiesf	73	106	292	315	23	121	390

a 18 months   b After deduction of the uncovered deficit in the Consumer Goods Account   c Including blocked aid amounting to 1,208 million drachmas in 1950/51 and 179 millions in 1952/53. Against this aid the Bank of Greece gave equivalent advances, settled out of the frozen U.S. aid counterpart funds according to the agreement concluded between the Bank of Greece and the government on November 30, 1955   d 854 million drachmas were released in 1952/53   e Converted into a long-term loan by the Bank of Greece, redeemable in annual instalments. Agreement signed between the Bank of Greece and the government on 23.10.63   f (+) denotes an increase in advances or a decrease in Treasury availabilities, (-) denotes a reduction in advances or a rise in availabilities   g Advances against blocked U.S. aid and N.A.T.O. special defense assistance   h Provisional data

117

TABLE 46

Public investment expenditure[a] 1951/52 through to 1963 by sectors
(in millions drachmas)

Sector	1950/51–1955/56		1957 — 1963[b]		1950/51–1963[b]	
	Amount	Per cent	Amount	Per cent	Amount	Per cent
Agriculture	2,190	19.9	12,605	28.3	14,795	26.7
Land improvement	Inadequate data		4,433	10.0	Inadequate data	
Other	»	»	8,172	18.3	»	»	»
Small public utility projects	245	2.2	3,149	7.0	3,394	6.1
Industry-power-mining	5,228	47.5	12,106	27.2	17,334	31.2
Power	2,758	25.0	6,633	14.9	9,391	16.9
Industry-other	2,470	22.5	5,473	12.3	7,943	14.3
Transport-telecommuni-cations	1,852	16.8	10,757	24.2	12,609	22.7
Roads and highways	763	6.9	5,966	13.4	6,729	12.1
Railways	404	3.7	1,097	2.5	1,501	2.7
Telecommunications	86	0.8	2,628	5.9	2,714	4.9
Other	599	5.4	1,066	2.4	1,685	3.0
Tourism	150	1.4	2,355	5.3	2,505	4.5
Education	309	2.8	876	2.0	1,185	2.1
Other and unallocated	1,030	9.4	2,622	6.0	3,652	6.7
Total	11,004	100.0	44,470	100.0	55,474	100.0

a Direct public investment under the central government investment program, the Public Power Corporation, the Greek Telecommunications Organization and the Workers' Housing Organization. Also, investment loans to the private sector by the Agricultural Bank, the Economic Development Financing Organization and the Workers' Housing Organization.
b Provisional data

Sources: For government investment in the years 1950/51, 1951/52 and 1952/53 : U.S.O.M., *Statistical Data Book 1954/55 and First Half of Fiscal Year 1955/56,* Volumes I and II, February 1956, Tables 125 (in Vol.II) and 51 (in Vol.I). For investment expenditure in 1953/54 and 1954/55 : "The Greek Economy in 1955 and 1956" by the Bank of Greece. For subsequent years: Ministry of Coordination. For investment by public entities, data have been supplied by the relevant enterprises and organizations.

banks as a compulsory financial investment of their private deposits—can be regarded as an important step towards placing the financing of public expenditure on a sounder basis. Short-term borrowing through treasury bills, while not an orthodox method for financing long-term investment, was indicated as a substitute for financing through Bank of Greece advances. To the extent that treasury bills were bought with commercial bank funds, credit was distributed between the private and public sectors in a manner better adjusted to the ability of each sector to use these funds productively. Whenever private investment activity failed to utilize total available credit, treasury bills made it possible for the government to use idle funds in order to increase its expenditure on investment.

Returns on public investment were, of course, influenced by the organizational weaknesses and limited technical know-how of the agencies involved. Nevertheless, it was preferable to increase even less productive forms of public investment rather than to allow funds to remain idle. Treasury bills also provided an additional instrument of monetary control, while from the fiscal standpoint, the substitution of short-term borrowing for central bank advances was a more healthy arrangement.

IV

BALANCE OF PAYMENTS POLICY

INTRODUCTION

External developments exert a decisive influence on [a developing country's rate of growth and monetary conditions. Since monetary stability, interpreted as a necessary condition of sustained economic development, embraces both internal and external stability, excessive inflationary pressures which are exported in the form of external deficits are very dangerous for the domestic economy. Persistent deficits in the balance of payments, aside from other detrimental effects, may undermine confidence as a result of the depletion of foreign exchange reserves. The existence of an adequate level of reserves is thus desirable not only to meet seasonal, cyclical, or unforeseen fluctuations in foreign receipts and payments, but also as a factor that strengthens confidence in the national currency. Therefore, substantial drains of foreign reserves may act as a stimulus to psychological inflation and may discourage potential capital inflows, even if relative price stability prevails at home.

Maintaining external equilibrium and relative price stability and achieving satisfactory rates of growth are the basic aims of economic policy in developing countries. Thus, to the extent that the provision and amount of aid granted by the advanced nations to developing countries are made to depend on the existence of balance-of-payments deficits in the latter, the countries extending the aid seem to encourage the neglect of external monetary equilibrium and to condone mismanagement in the external sector. The balance of payments position and, especially, the level of foreign exchange reserves, when taken as exclusive criteria, are frequently misleading for a sound evaluation of a developing country's actual economic aid requirements.

BALANCE OF PAYMENTS

The external sector of an economy is not just the passive receiver of internal inflationary pressures, it also exerts a decisive influence on the course of development and the degree of monetary stability that prevails at home. The foreign sector should, therefore, be watched carefully by the authorities of a developing country and policies at home should be adjusted in a way that takes full account of foreign price developments. In fact, the limits imposed by the balance of payments have become more flexible as a result of the creeping inflation which characterized the advanced economies in the postwar period. This, however, does not mean that developments in the international economy have been generally favorable to underdeveloped countries.

Equilibrium in the balance of payments has been a matter of serious concern for most developing countries and in many cases the short-term dilemma between a higher rate of development and monetary stability has been a pressing one. Given the close interrelation between growth and stability in the longer run, it becomes clear that the developing economies can escape from this dilemma if they are effectively assisted by the advanced countries in their efforts to expand and diversify exports. It should be borne in mind that in many cases the loss of earnings from fluctuating exports is equal to or greater than the amount of aid given to a developing country. Clearly, a solution to this pressing problem can be found only in greater cooperation between industrial and primary producing countries. This cooperation should also extend to the field of capital inflows to developing countries and should ensure them an adequate provision of investment capital. It should be stressed that the continued expansion of world trade and the stability of the international monetary system depends crucially on the ability and willingness of industrial countries to run deficits on capital account on a sufficient scale to sustain an adequate rate of growth in the countries in process of development.

The Greek balance of trade has been characterized by

121

chronic deficits. Despite the improvement which has taken place in recent years in the over-all balance of payments, a fundamental and ever-widening deficit in the balance of trade still remains the central problem of commercial policy. Greek exports showed a considerable increase following the 1953 devaluation, but have risen at a very slow rate since the mid-fifties. This slow development is not unrelated to the increasingly difficult market conditions under which Greek exports have had to compete, especially in countries of multi-lateral settlement. On the other hand, the pattern of Greek exports has not shown any marked improvement. As indicated in Table 55, exports of industrial products account for only 4 per cent of total exports and at times have even fallen below that percentage, while agricultural products have maintained their share, the only changes in their composition worth singling out, as new and dynamic export items being cotton and fruit. In general, both the volume and the value of exports constitute one of the most fundamental problems of the Greek economy. A substantial increase in exports is of vital importance, not only from the point of view of external equilibrium, but also because it will set in motion a process of modernization and rationalization of economic activity.

Giving an export orientation to the country's productive capacity is of particular importance for industrial products in view of the need to promote industrialization and the favorable tariff treatment of industrial exports within the E.E.C. In fact since summer 1963, Greek industrial exports to the E.E.C. countries are subject to lower duties (60 per cent less than previously); even these duties will be abolished altogether in the course of the next few years under the tariff elimination program for Community members. On the other hand, a sufficiently long transition period has been granted to Greek industry in the home market. Thus, duties on industrial imports from the E.E.C. will be gradually abolished over a period of 22 years for products that were

122

manufactured in Greece at the end of 1962 and 12 years for items that were not manufactured locally at that time, these periods starting from the date on which the E.E.C.-Greece Association Agreement first came into force, i.e. November 1, 1962.

However, the emphasis given to the effort to expand industrial exports in no way detracts from the important task of promoting Greek agricultural exports. A stronger effort must be made to improve the quality of traditional export products and to add new items to the export list by readjusting crop structure. The favorable conditions established by the Association Agreement for the major agricultural exports of Greece to E.E.C. countries should assist this effort.

Greek imports have increased at a rapid rate during the last decade. Following the 1953 liberalization, import payments rose from $236.1 million in 1953 to $708.4 million in 1963, an increase which cannot be entirely explained by income changes. A liberal import policy has been pursued since 1953 in the belief that competition in foreign trade, despite the risks it may involve for development, in the last analysis provides necessary incentives and sound conditions for a sustained process of development. This policy of free trade does not imply that the responsible authorities should divest themselves of all and any power to control both the volume and the pattern of imports.

The consideration of imports as a magnitude which is basically determined by the propensity to import could lead to overlooking the fact that imports in a developing economy are not only a result of the increase in income but act also as one of the important prerequisites for such an increase. To the extent that imports consist of capital and basic consumer goods, they are of fundamental significance for the rate of growth of income. In this context, it has been argued that once the total value of imports is at a level which conforms to external equilibrium requirements, their

123

structure should be freely determined by the market on the basis of comparative advantage for the economy. According to this view, the dominant position of consumer goods in the import bill will not have adverse effects on development since it implies a corresponding release of productive resources at home, which can be used for the investment needs of development. However, it has repeatedly been pointed out that the low level of technical and organizational ability, the deficient working of the price mechanism in less-developed countries, and the inadequacy of private initiative in general, render the second part of the above argument of dubious validity.

It is therefore necessary for the responsible authorities to exert a systematic influence on the pattern of imports through monetary credit and fiscal policies without, of course, disregarding the fundamental principle of free trade.

Greece has been able to meet her widening trade deficit and to maintain her rate of growth through the substantial surpluses on the balance of invisibles, and the inflow of capital. (This is especially the case for the post-1952 period, after the drastic cut in U.S. aid.) To a considerable degree, these favorable developments were the result of the restoration and maintenance of monetary equilibrium. Monetary policy and the level of imports would both have been fundamentally different if the authorities had not made a correct estimate of the steadily increasing inflow of invisible receipts and foreign capital. It can be maintained, therefore, that the deficit in the trade balance was not a phenomenon beyond the control of the authorities, but a regular consequence of developments in the balance of invisibles and the capital account.

It is hardly encouraging to find that some advanced countries consider a strong foreign exchange position a disqualification for the receipt of economic assistance. Such considerations do not provide an incentive to prudent financial policies on the part of developing countries. Moreover, in many cases the volume of foreign exchange reserves is not by itself a reliable indicator of a country's foreign liquidity position, and this is true for Greece. When judging Greek external aid requirements, the level and trend of the foreign exchange reserves are particularly misleading if considered in isolation. A correct estimate of Greece's liquidity position should take into account her foreign short-term liabilities and particularly suppliers' credits, which have increased at a fast pace in the last few years.

TABLE 47

Foreign exchange reserves and suppliers' credits, 1950–1963
(in millions U.S. dollars)

	Foreign exchange reserves (end of year total)	Suppliers' credits (outstanding total at year's end)
1950	54.4	—
1951	56.2	—
1952	71.9	—
1953	120.6	7.2
1954	131.5	16.1
1955	186.8	28.9
1956	190.1	53.5
1957	178.9	87.3
1958	161.7	105.1
1959	207.6	101.1
1960	223.5	108.9
1961	250.5	114.9
1962	269.9	146.7
1963	277.9	169.9

Source: Bank of Greece.

As can be seen in Table 47, the net liquidity position of the Greek economy does not justify the view that an extraordinary increase in exchange reserves has taken place. Moreover, a fairly substantial part of the increase in foreign reserves represents the proceeds of postwar loans, the servicing of which will impose a real burden on the Greek economy in the near future.

It should also be noted that the use of foreign loans instead of grants in aid to cover defense expenditures of largely supranational importance would have extremely adverse effects on the growth rate of the Greek economy and would amount to a disheartening appraisal of the efforts made by Greece.

THE BALANCE OF PAYMENTS DURING THE 1950-1963 PERIOD

The restoration of equilibrium in the Greek balance of payments

Up to 1952, the external transactions of Greece were marked by a basic imbalance reflecting the fact that normal conditions had not yet been restored in the country's productive capacity and that inflation persisted as a dominant force. The deficit on current account was covered almost entirely from U.S. aid, which was adjusted approximately to the amount of the deficit. In 1952, when U.S. foreign aid policy was revised and the amounts granted to Greece were sharply reduced, a drastic reduction was made in imports to face this situation and a series of counter-inflationary measures was adopted. A more radical step towards placing Greek external transactions on a sounder basis and restoring equilibrium in the balance of payments was taken in 1953, when the drachma was devalued by 50 per cent and imports were liberalized. This radical measure was combined with serious efforts to achieve monetary stability in order to create conditions conducive to the development of the country's foreign exchange resources and to establish balance of payments equilibrium at a foreign exchange expenditure level almost twice as high as that of 1950. From some $280 million in 1950 the annual deficit on current account has been reduced since 1956 to between $56 million and $88 million, i.e., a yearly average

126

of $74 million for the whole period (1956–1963). The final deficit before aid amounted to $274 million |in 1950 and decreased to an annual average of $38 million between 1955 and 1958, while in 1961 there was a slight surplus of $1.2 million, in 1962 a small deficit of $2.7 million, and in 1963 a considerable surplus of $19.2 million.

TABLE 48

Development of the balance of payments, 1950–1963
(in millions U.S. dollars)

Year	Balance on current account	Balance of payments deficits and surpluses before aid
1950	—278.8	—274.1
1951	—287.1	—279.6
1952	—113.3	—108.5
1953	— 17.6	— 12.7
1954	— 64.5	— 46.0
1955	— 27.7	— 3.6
1956	— 87.9	— 67.9
1957	— 66.3	— 36.6
1958	— 78.8	— 42.0
1959	— 60.0	— 2.0
1960	— 80.8	— 32.3
1961	— 83.4	+ 1.2
1962	— 73.9	— 2.7
1963	— 56.1	+ 19.2

Source: Bank of Greece.

The currency devaluation of 1953 eliminated the fundamental disparity between domestic and international prices and made possible an expansion of exports within the limits of the country's productive capacity for exportable goods under the existing economic structure, and led to an increase in invisible receipts and the inflow of capital. Since then, the restoration of internal monetary equilibrium has enabled the maintenance of a measure of correspondence between international and domestic prices and thus eliminated an obstacle to the further growth of foreign exchange earnings. The relatively slight rise in the Greek price level since 1956 has been smaller than that of most European countries.

The conditions created by the favorable development of the price level made it possible to stimulate the growth of the country's foreign exchange receipts through specific economic policy measures, which facilitated export activity and the inflow of invisibles and capital. Throughout this period, a favorable factor was the substantial and almost continuous growth of the international economy. Although the rapid rise in income abroad has not markedly affected Greek exports because their composition is dominated by products of low income elasticity of demand, it has nevertheless played a considerable role in the development of invisible receipts, in particular tourism, emigrants' remittances, and foreign exchange earnings from shipping.

The policy objective of safeguarding external economic equilibrium was also evident in measures designed to have an indirect effect on imports, as further analyzed below. Import quotas were removed by Greece to an extent paralleled at the time by only a few European countries, and this was definitely a decisive factor in restoring sound conditions in the country's external transactions. However, some control over the total volume and composition of imports was needed, especially in order to influence the structure of aggregate national expenditure towards the basic aim of economic development. The recommendations made by representatives of the International Monetary Fund to the effect that import controls should be lifted completely, have tended to underestimate the fact that Greek foreign trade policy is—*ceteris paribus*—one of the least restrictive in Europe, and also the restraining influence which excessive imports of consumer goods would exert on the

128

development of the Greek economy.

The adjustment of the exchange rate and the gradual stabilization of the domestic price level eliminated a basic obstacle to capital inflow and invisible receipts. The country's improved economic position had a favorable influence on all sources of invisible receipts, especially on some categories of invisibles which were related more closely to developments within Greece itself, e.g., tourism. Economic progress was also important to the fairly satisfactory development of capital inflow and to the increase in earnings from shipping activities, as it contributed to induce Greek shipowners to adopt the Greek flag.

The favorable effect of improved economic conditions on the development of invisible receipts and capital inflow was further stimulated by special measures and incentives. One of the most important measures was the favorable tax and foreign exchange regime established for ships hoisting the Greek flag and the protection and tax incentives given to foreign investment, particularly in the export and mining sectors, as well as to domestic enterprises which manufacture import substitutes.

Lastly, in order to attract short-term capital, certain banks—as specified from time to time—were authorized to accept deposits in foreign exchange. These deposits are withdrawable after a minimum period of six months and can be made by Greeks or foreigners permanently residing abroad, or by corporations established outside Greece.

Balance of invisibles

During the period under review, there have been particularly favorable developments in the economic activity of the countries of destination of Greek emigrants, and in international tourism. The combination of a more stable economic climate and propitious external conditions led to a very rapid increase in invisible receipts, especially after 1953.

129

Within the 1950–1963 period these receipts increased eightfold, while the net surplus on invisibles rose almost twelve times.

TABLE 49

Balance of invisibles
(in millions U.S. dollars)

Year	Invisible receipts	Invisible payments	Surplus on invisibles
1950	55.2	24.8	30.4
1951	62.9	25.9	37.0
1952	74.4	25.6	48.8
1953	107.8	23.4	84.4
1954	124.2	30.1	94.1
1955	153.8	36.0	117.8
1956	182.6	39.4	143.2
1957	235.7	49.7	186.0
1958	217.6	47.7	169.9
1959	237.2	54.9	182.3
1960	273.2	65.5	207.7
1961	319.6	76.1	243.5
1962	379.6	87.6	292.0
1963	454.3	97.9	356.4

Source: Bank of Greece.

The rate of increase in the various categories of invisible receipts changed frequently during the period under consideration and caused structural changes which are reflected in the larger share of receipts from tourism and shipping in recent years.

TABLE 50

Percentage breakdown of invisible receipts

	1954	1955	1956	1957	1958	1959	1960	1961	1962	1963
Emigrants' remittances	37.8	32.9	33.4	31.8	35.3	37.4	33.1	30.8	30.9	28.2
Transport (shipping)	22.6	23.1	26.4	28.3	27.7	25.4	28.0	31.9	28.6	27.6
Foreign travel	20.4	18.9	17.1	17.6	16.6	17.6	18.1	19.5	20.0	21.0
Government	...	...	10.2	8.0	10.6	8.8	9.4	5.4	5.5	4.0
Other	19.2	25.1	12.9	14.3	9.8	10.8	11.4	12.4	15.0	19.2
	100.0	100.0	100.0	100.0	100.0	100.0	100.0	100.0	100.0	100.0

Source: Bank of Greece.

130

The rapid rise in invisible receipts resulted in a gradual increase in their share in the financing of imports. In fact, since 1961 net invisible receipts have exceeded earnings from exports.

TABLE 51

Percentage of imports financed by invisible receipts and by export earnings

Year	Net invisible receipts	Exports	Total
1938	30.4	65.9	96.3
1950	7.7	21.5	29.2
1953	33.7	56.8	90.5
1954	29.4	50.4	79.8
1955	33.4	58.7	92.1
1956	32.4	47.5	79.9
1957	39.1	46.9	86.0
1958	34.6	49.4	84.0
1959	40.1	46.7	86.8
1960	41.8	42.0	83.8
1961	43.4	41.7	85.1
1962	48.0	39.9	87.9
1963	50.3	41.8	92.1

Source: Bank of Greece.

The high rate of increase in invisible receipts, which continued throughout the period under review, shows that they are a dynamic source of foreign exchange for Greece and provides ground for an optimistic outlook. It should not be overlooked, however, that the external factors determining invisible receipts cannot be influenced by domestic economic policy and are liable to fluctuations. However, under the postwar conditions of international economic cooperation, it is unlikely that international economic activity —which has an influence on international tourism—will be marked by sharp changes, such as would have an adverse effect on the development of Greek invisible receipts and cause serious disturbances in the country's balance of payments. This could happen, however, in the case of international political crises or other disruptive developments which would have an appreciable impact not only on most of the basic categories of invisible receipts but also on exports and capital inflow.

Capital movements

The annual net inflow of capital increased over fifteen times during the period under review. Although this was of great assistance in balancing the country's foreign payments, economic policy aims regarding the utilization of imported funds were not fully achieved. In fact, the capital that flowed into Greece on the basis of Law 2687/53, which provides incentives for productive investment conducive to economic development, represented only 13 per cent of the total capital inflow in the last five years.

Over the last two years, however, the sharp rise in the amount of imported capital, together with the faster pace at which applications for approval of capital imports were submitted to the Greek authorities, indicate that the trend of foreign investment in this country will be much more favorable in the future. It should also be remembered that, irrespective of its weaknesses, the policy introduced in 1953 and subsequent legislation to attract foreign investors could not be expected to have any immediate results. This phenomenon is observed in all developing economies. In the postwar years, investors have shown a marked preference for investing their capital in industrial countries, and have only shown an interest in underdeveloped areas of the world in certain special fields such as petroleum. A far-reaching effort is therefore needed to eliminate the reluctance of foreign investors, who are influenced in their decisions by several factors and particularly by their lack of confidence in the political and economic stability of underdeveloped countries. In Greece, over-all economic progress and the

132

monetary stability achieved during the period under review have removed the grounds for such distrust. A continuous effort is being made to create still better conditions which will have a decisive effect in attracting foreign capital and entrepreneurship towards productive activities in Greece.

IMPORT POLICY AND THE PROBLEM OF EXPORTS

Imports

It has already been mentioned that the abolition of import quotas, in conjunction with the devaluation of the drachma in 1953, was a major factor in the establishment of monetary equilibrium.

After 1953, however, economic policy had to cope with the problem of maintaining imports within reasonable limits, inasmuch as the abolition of quotas was followed by a very large import expansion. Moreover, the rise in imports was facilitated by favorable conditions in terms of suppliers' credit which enabled the continuing expansion of sales on credit.

The prevention of an excessive expansion in imports was sought through measures designed to reduce the rate of increase in certain categories of imports. Such a reduction helped to maintain the total volume of these imports within reasonable limits and ensured that their structure would be better geared to the needs of economic development. The measures taken for this purpose included credit, tariffs, and taxes in general. Credit measures were aimed mainly at differentiating the terms of bank credit to the import trade by basic commodity categories, each of which was treated according to its importance to the development process. Differentiation was also made in the procedures required in import approval and payment.

During 1953, imports showed a considerable decline, which was due to a sharp increase in the cost of imported goods as a result of the devaluation. After 1953, however, the

133

newly adopted import liberalization policy resulted in a rapid expansion of imports, which in 1954 alone increased by 35 per cent. By 1955, the expansion of imports had reached a point where it became necessary to adopt measures that would have an indirect contractionary influence on imports of luxuries and non-basic commodities, particularly those which were also manufactured in Greece. These measures included the shortening of the time limit for customs clearance, the introduction of advance deposits against bills of lading covering between 15 and 100 per cent of the value of imported goods, restrictions on credit for importing non-basic commodities, etc. A relative slackening in the rate of increase in imports was achieved through these measures, although the rate remained quite high (10 per cent). Some of these measures were later somewhat relaxed, e.g., the time limit for customs clearance of a number of basic commodities, and a longer period of time was allowed for settling payments of raw materials. In 1958, the accelerating expansion of imports necessitated certain adjustments in the prevailing system of import regulations. The new measures were considered necessary in order to influence imports according to the aims of over-all economic development policy. To satisfy basic consumer needs and the increasing requirements for producer equipment and raw materials, it was imperative that the rise in imports of nonessential and luxury goods should be kept within certain limits. The following measures were therefore adopted :

First, the time limit allowed for settling payments of imported goods was shortened—except in the case of raw materials and machinery—and the advance deposits made upon the issuance of import licences were increased, in order to slow down the rate of increase in imports of nonessential commodities.

Second, nonessential imported and domestic goods were made subject to consumer sales-taxes, and the tax for licenc-

134

ing a passenger car was raised by a substantial amount. Finally, in 1959, it became necessary to take a number of measures to deal with the problem of the continuously widening trade gap with the area of multilateral settlement and with Europe in particular. Quotas were applied on imports of certain categories of products, and some imported consumer goods were made subject to special licence, etc. These measures proved effective in containing or reducing imports of the specified commodities and, to some extent, they contributed to the decline in the total volume of imports in 1959, which occurred for the first time since 1954. This decline was also caused by other factors of a more or less permanent nature, such as the reduced need for the import of basic foodstuffs resulting from an increase in domestic production. Furthermore, it appears also to have been due to a considerable extent to the reduction in stocks of imported raw materials in 1959. These stocks had increased excessively in 1958, owing to a decline in their prices.

After 1959, the trend of imports and over-all developments in the Greek balance of payments allowed for a more liberal import policy. Thus, import quotas were abolished in 1960, and a series of measures were taken in 1961 to give greater freedom to the import trade. In 1962, the time limit for settling payments under foreign suppliers' credit was increased from 6 to 12 months, and a three-year settlement period was allowed on imports of mechanical equipment and spare parts. When the Association Agreement was brought into force on November 1, 1962, tariffs on imports from the E.E.C. countries were lowered by 5 per cent for goods which are also manufactured in Greece and by 10 per cent for those not produced in Greece. These reductions were followed on May 1, 1964, by a further 10 per cent reduction of duties on E.E.C. products imported into Greece and not manufactured locally. Other measures liberalizing imports were also introduced, such as the reduction of advance deposits required for some types of merchandise, which were also extended to goods imported from countries outside the E.E.C.

Under the influence of the policy pursued during the 13-year period, the structure of imports underwent several changes, corresponding to developments in domestic production. As can be seen from Table 52, the share of foodstuffs, fuels, and lubricants in total imports decreased as a result of increasing domestic production, while capital goods and manufactured consumer goods increased their share in the total. These changes reflect both intensified investment activity and greater consumption of imported manufactures as a result of the economic upswing and the improved standard of living of the population.

TABLE 52

Import structure
(on a payment basis, percentages)

	1952	1957	1958	1959	1960	1961	1962	1963
I. Foodstuffs	21.3	19.4	16.0	15.6	18.8	17.8	14.0	18.6
II. Raw materials	28.0	27.0	25.9	25.5	26.5	25.0	24.9	23.4
III. Fuels-lubricants	14.3	12.7	9.5	11.3	9.6	8.4	7.9	7.3
IV. Capital goods	12.6	11.2	18.0	18.2	15.7	17.8	22.3	18.9
V. Manufactured consumer goods	19.7	27.3	28.6	29.1	29.4	31.0	30.9	31.6
VI. Freight (unallocated)	4.1	2.4	2.0	0.3	—	—	—	0.2
	100.0	100.0	100.0	100.0	100.0	100.0	100.0	100.0

Source: Bank of Greece, Foreign Exchange Statistics.

As can be seen in Table 53, the rate of increase in consumer goods imports since 1956 has been higher than that of total domestic consumption. The rate of increase was also high in the case of producer goods imports, when compared with gross fixed capital investment at home.

136

BALANCE OF PAYMENTS

TABLE 53

Consumption, investment, and imports
(in real terms)

Indices : 1954=100

Year	Total domestic consumption	Imports of con- sumer goods [a]	Gross investment (excluding ships)	Imports of pro- ducer goods [a] [b]
1954	100.0	100.0	100.0	100.0
1955	104.1	111.6	114.8	120.4
1956	112.2	124.0	132.3	146.2
1957	120.4	135.2	134.7	178.5
1958	123.4	147.4	178.0	232.7
1959	127.1	133.6	178.3	211.5
1960	132.9	149.6	204.7	234.4
1961	144.5	169.4	232.9	275.0
1962	152.4	180.7	252.9	318.1
1963	163.0[c]	225.6	268.7[c]	324.1

[a] Imports on the basis of arrivals
[b] Including imports of machinery, transport equipment (except private cars) and construction materials. Excluding ships
[c] Provisional estimates
  Sources: Ministry of Coordination, National Statistical Service of Greece.

Significant achievements were: first, the maintenance of total expenditure on imports within limits that did not endanger the country's external equilibrium, yet allowed for continuous economic progress; and, second, the improvement in the structure of imports indicated by the far higher rate of increase in producer goods imports, as compared with the rate for imports of consumer goods.

Exports

After the considerable rise in exports in 1954 and 1955 under the influence of the currency devaluation, further export expansion came to depend on over-all economic

137

progress at home and particularly on the rate at which structural changes were being effected in domestic production. Special policy measures to improve exports could only have a limited effect under the given structure of the economy and this explains the slow rate of increase in exports after 1955—especially in comparison to the rate of export expansion on an international scale during the same period—and their declining share in financing imports.

TABLE 54

Exports of Mediterranean countries
(1955=100)

Country	1956	1957	1958	1959	1960	1961	1962
Egypt	98	118	114	110	136	116	97
GREECE	104	104	120	127	111	122	136
Israel	118	155	155	197	238	269	307
Italy	116	137	139	157	197	225	251
Lebanon	121	127	94	121	127	124	194
Portugal	105	101	101	102	115	114	130
Spain	99	107	109	112	163	159	165
Syria	103	111	84	81	83	76	120
Turkey	97	110	79	113	103	111	122
Yugoslavia	126	154	172	186	220	221	268
World exports	111	119	114	121	135	141	148

Source: I.M.F., *International Financial Statistics.*

The composition of Greek exports is a basic obstacle to their expansion. Approximately 75 per cent of Greek exports consist of a few agricultural products of low income elasticity of demand. Furthermore, most of the dynamic export products of Greece (e.g. fruits and vegetables) are handicapped by the policies of several importing countries, which periodically apply quantitative restrictions on imports to protect their own producers, or extend more favorable treatment to the products of areas with which they have closer ties.

TABLE 55

Structure of Greek exports, 1952-1963

Category	1952	1954	1956	1958	1960	1961	1962	1963
Agric. produce	76.8	74.7	69.3	82.0	74.4	74.9	74.8	81.0
Tobacco	46.1	37.6	30.8	37.9	34.7	34.4	28.0	43.2
Cotton	3.0	6.6	13.7	9.5	9.2	11.7	16.1	11.5
Currants	17.7	14.9	12.9	14.4	13.1	12.5	11.7	11.1
Olives and olive oil	2.5	8.1	2.0	4.4	5.4	2.2	4.3	3.2
Fruit	1.2	1.9	3.3	3.5	5.1	6.7	7.8	5.6
Other	6.3	5.6	6.6	12.3	6.9	7.4	6.9	6.4
Ores	9.0	5.2	8.4	6.1	8.6	6.7	6.4	5.3
Industrial and handi-craft products	4.6	1.9	1.2	2.1	3.7	3.4	4.5	3.3
N.A.T.O. commodities	—	5.2	7.4	1.9	2.3	3.3	2.4	0.4
Other	9.6	13.0	13.7	7.9	11.0	11.7	11.9	10.0
Colophony-Turpentine	2.8	2.7	3.4	1.6	3.5	3.4	2.0	0.8
Leather, hides, skins	2.5	2.2	2.5	2.7	4.5	4.6	4.1	3.3
Printed matter, cine-films, etc.	4.3	8.1	7.8	3.6	3.0	3.7	5.8	5.9
	100.0	100.0	100.0	100.0	100.0	100.0	100.0	100.0

Source: Bank of Greece.

The share of industrial products in total Greek exports remained very low throughout the period under review. This is clearly shown by comparing Greek industrial exports with those of other countries, most of which are broadly at the same stage of economic development.

TABLE 56

Percentage share of industrial exports in total exports of selected countries

	1955	1956	1957	1958	1959	1960	1961	1962
Bulgaria	...	...	38	36	33	30	...	...
Egypt	7	14	13	8	13	...	...	...
GREECE	7	8	6	7	7	10	10	11
Ireland	12	12	14	14	18	19	18	20
Israel	54	50	55	52	58	62	65	...
Italy	71	72	71	74	76	74	75	75
Lebanon	39	35	36	36	41	...	...	...
Portugal	42	45	48	47	50	52	53	55
Spain	26	29	28	27	31	31	31	30
Syria	10	11	14	16	18	18	14	...
Turkey	4	7	3	4	3	6	3	3
Yugoslavia	39	42	46	44	52	50	50	56

Note: The above Table is based on the S.I.T.C. Therefore, the share of Greek industrial exports does not agree with the percentage based on foreign exchange statistics, as the S.I.T.C. includes resin products (regarded as chemicals), books, newspapers, etc.

Sources: U.N., *International Trade Statistics,* O.E.C.D., *Trade by Commodities,* Vol. I.

Several measures were taken to promote Greek export trade by expanding domestic production and improving its structure. Throughout the period under review, Greek export trade was granted many credit facilities. In particular, since 1959, all restrictions on credit to this sector have been lifted, and interest rates have been substantially reduced. New incentives to promote exports, especially of industrial and handicraft products, were introduced in 1962. These measures aimed at the differential treatment of enterprises in terms of financing and interest rates, according to their export performance. Export expansion was also encouraged through the provision of various facilities, such as tax reductions or exemptions, tax allowances on gross earnings, and increased depreciation rates.

V

MONEY INCOMES

INTRODUCTION

The relation between the rates of increase in the volume of production on one hand and aggregate money incomes on the other occupies a central position in the analysis of inflation and in the formulation of monetary policy. A higher rate of increase in money incomes than in production creates excess purchasing power in the hands of the public and leads, as a rule, to inflation. Inflationary pressures are reflected in higher prices (and, usually, wages) and increased imports (and, possibly, reduced exports).

The present chapter attempts two things: first, to estimate the excess increases in money incomes in Greece during the period 1951–1963 as a whole, and for the periods 1951–1956 and 1957–1963 taken separately; second, to identify the causes of these excess increases in money incomes.

AN ESTIMATE OF THE INCREASE IN MONEY INCOME IN
    EXCESS OF THE TOTAL SUPPLY OF GOODS AND
    SERVICES DURING 1951–1963

Between 1951 and 1963, aggregate money expenditure increased by 58.2 billion drachmas over the total supply of goods and services. This excess in money expenditure corresponds to an inflationary increase in money incomes, which is analyzed below by income groups for the period 1951–1963 as a whole, and for the periods 1951–1956 and 1957–1963.

As can be seen in Table 57, 24 per cent of the increase in expenditure beyond available goods and services contributed to an inflationary increase in agricultural incomes, 31 per cent constituted an inflationary increase in income from property and business, 28 per cent represents an increase

141

TABLE 57

Analysis of excess expenditure between 1951 and 1963[a]

	1951–1963[b]		1951–1956		1957–1963	
	Billion drs.	Per cent	Billion drs.	Per cent	Billion drs.	Per cent
Excess expenditure[c]	58.2	100.0	30.0	100.0	11.7	100.0
Absorbed by :						
a. Agricultural income	13.9	23.9	8.8	29.2	2.3	19.9
b. Wages and salaries	16.2	27.8	9.3	31.0	0.8	7.1
c. Business profits	17.9	30.7	7.4	24.7	5.6	47.7
(of which rents)[d]	(3.7)	(6.3)	(1.9)	(6.3)	(0.1)	(0.8)
d. Income from property and business activities of the state[e]	1.4	2.5	0.3	1.3	0.8	6.9
e. Indirect taxes	6.4	10.9	2.7	8.8	1.8	15.8
f. Changes in the prices of imports	2.4	4.2	1.5	5.0	0.3	2.6

a The analysis of Table 57 has been made on the basis of the method employed by the Council on Prices, Productivity and Incomes in the U.K. It is not comparable with that of Table 15, which shows changes in excess demand on an annual basis

b The data for 1951–56 and 1957–63 do not add up with those for the whole period since estimates for those two periods were made on the basis of 1951 and 1956 prices respectively, whereas those for the whole period were made on the basis of 1951 prices

c Excess expenditure is the increase in gross expenditure above the increase in total supply of goods and services

d Includes income from state property

e Net income

Source: *National Accounts of Greece, 1948–1959.* Data for 1963 have been taken from the National Accounts Division of the Ministry of Coordination.

in wages and salaries and 11 per cent an increase in indirect taxes. Finally, 4 per cent of the increase in expenditure was absorbed by higher import prices.

It would be useful to consider in some detail the course

142

of money incomes in relation to changes in domestic production and productivity. This is attempted below for the period 1951–1963.

The average annual rate of increase in domestic production (i.e., gross national income at constant factor cost) during the period 1951–1963 was 6.3 per cent (see Table 58). Money incomes (i.e., gross national income at current factor cost) as a whole increased during the same period at an average annual rate of 11.5 per cent.

The increase in money incomes at a considerably higher rate than production signifies that strong inflationary forces were at work during this period. However, there was a difference in the intensity of these pressures during the two sub-periods. During the first part of the period under review (i.e., 1951–1956) inflationary pressures were quite strong. Money incomes increased at an average annual rate of 16.8 per cent while domestic production increased at an average annual rate of 6.2 per cent. The second part of the period (1957–1963) is characterized by relative price stability, with money incomes rising at an annual average rate of 7.3 per cent and domestic production increasing at the slightly lower rate of 6.4 per cent.

It is worth noting that throughout the period profits and income from property increased at a faster rate than wages and salaries. Moreover, if the remuneration of company directors is removed from the income group of "wages and salaries" and placed in "profits," then the rate of increase in the latter category will be higher than the one given in Table 58. (This manipulation of company directors' income is justifiable in view of the family nature of most companies in Greece. Managers are frequently the owners of the companies they direct). Finally, it should be noted that agricultural incomes rose at a slower rate than non-agricultural incomes throughout the 1951–1963 period.

From Table 58, it would appear that no major change has taken place in the relative shares of the five groups. It is

143

TABLE 58

Average annual change of domestic production and money incomes
in the period 1951–1963

| | Average annual change | | | Percentage distribution | | |
	1951–63	1951–56	1957–63	1951	1956	1963
		per cent				
Aggregate money income a	11.5	16.8	7.3	100.0	100.0	100.0
1. Agricultural income	9.9	16.1	5.4	34.6	32.9	27.8
2. Wages, salaries	11.6	16.8	7.8	35.7	36.2	36.4
3. Business profits	13.5	18.2	10.1	29.3	30.2	34.9
(of which rents) b	(17.7)	(28.4)	(10.1)	3.2	(5.1)	(5.9)
4. Income from property and business activity of the State c	22.5	37.1	12.1	0.4	0.7	0.9
Domestic production d	6.3	6.2	6.4			

a Gross national income at current factor cost
b Includes income from property of the State
c Net income
d Gross national income at constant factor cost

Source: *National Accounts of Greece, 1948–59* and *1958–62*. Data
for 1963 have been taken from the National Accounts Division of the
Ministry of Coordination.

not possible, however, to arrive at a definite conclusion
regarding income redistribution among the five groups
unless account is taken of the changes in employment and
active population that must have taken place during the
relevant period. Such data on the Greek economy are not
available in a comprehensive and sufficiently reliable form.

THE CAUSES OF THE EXCESS INCREASE IN MONEY INCOMES

The foregoing analysis has shown that the period from 1951
to 1963 was characterized by inflationary increases in money
incomes, which were quite substantial in the first six years of

the period and relatively limited after 1957. The course of prices and incomes since 1951 cannot be attributed to a single cause, since both demand and cost elements have contributed with varying force to the inflationary pressures prevailing in the 1950's. Although it is extremely difficult, if not impossible, to separate the influence that each factor had on a given inflationary situation, we will attempt a rough assessment of the role played by demand and cost factors.

Excess demand

Inflationary pressures prevailed throughout the 1950's. This was only to be expected in a developing country such as Greece, where the effort to accelerate the rate of growth necessitates a level of investment expenditure which often exceeds available domestic savings. Moreover, under the influence of the international demonstration effect, the population of developing countries continuously presses for consumption levels which exceed available productive capacity.

In the Greek case, the main factors making for excess demand in the period 1951 to 1963, and especially in the early part of the period, were the following:

First, the high marginal propensity to consume, due to several factors including the satisfaction of a large backlog of demand, generated during the war period and its aftermath. Furthermore, inflationary pressures were intensified by the strong propensity of the public to purchase goods as a hedge against inflation.

Second, another source of excess demand before 1956 was the large budget deficits, which were the result of substantial defense and social relief expenditures. In these circumstances, it became necessary to cover part of the consumption expenditures of the public sector by issuing notes, a course that contributed to the inflationary increase in money incomes.

145

The financing of private-sector requirements by central bank credits was a third cause of inflationary pressures. For instance, Bank of Greece advances from the note-issue covered some 68 per cent of total lending to the private sector in 1950 and 48 per cent in 1955. Thus, despite rigorous controls in force at the time, the credit mechanism was an important source of inflationary pressures.

Finally, an important cause of inflationary pressures in the 1950's was the extension of the installment credit system over a wide area of the economy. This system makes possible the discounting of future incomes and thus permits an increase of consumption spending in the present. To the extent that the net amount of outstanding debt increases, excess demand is thus usually created, which results in higher prices or increased imports. Available data from the Currency Committee records indicate, for example, that whereas total sales of 30 large industrial firms increased by 39 per cent between 1958–1963, their sales on installment credit increased by 51 per cent over the same period.

The inflationary trends generated by the above factors gradually subsided under the influence of coordinated fiscal and monetary measures.

Costs of production

The continuous rise in demand made a substantial contribution to inflationary increases in money incomes, especially during the first part of the 1951–1963 period, when inflationary pressures were fed by serious fiscal deficits and by the inflationary financing of the economy. In some cases, rising prices were the result of increased costs of production. On the side of costs, the main factors which contributed to inflationary pressures in the period under review are analyzed below.

During the period of strong inflation it was natural for labor unions to relate their claims for higher wages to rises

146

in the cost of living index. In the early part of the period up to 1950, the cost of living index rose rapidly, but in the unsettled conditions then prevailing, efforts by labor unions to obtain a comparable adjustment in wage rates were without effect. When, after 1950, political conditions came back to normal, workers in their claims for higher wages sought not only to compensate actual price rises, but also to recover part of the real income lost in the severe inflation of the pre-1950 period. This attitude largely accounts

DIAGRAM 7

Percentage changes in wages, cost of living, and output per worker indices

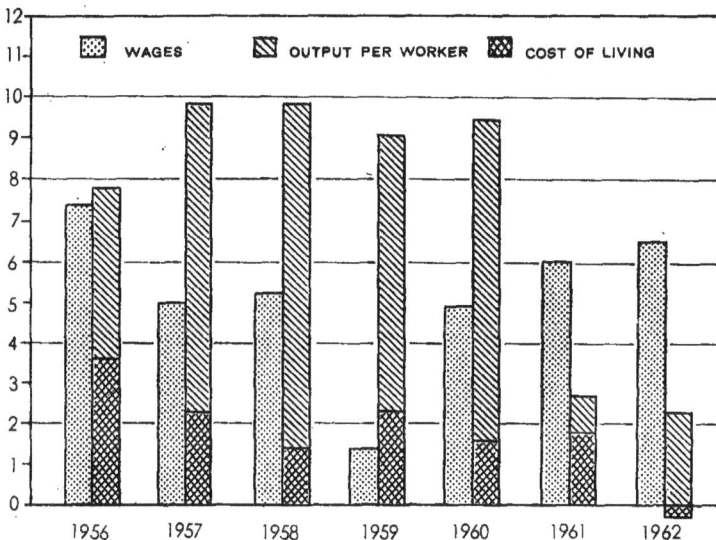

for the fact that, whereas the average annual rise in the cost of living index between 1950 and 1956 was only 8.5 per cent, minimum wage rates increased at an average annual rate of 15 per cent. After 1957, coordinated monetary and fiscal measures, together with import liberalization, brought about a relative stability in the price level. Wage claims, however, continued to be put forward. The aim now was to secure a

147

rising standard of living by pressing wage claims which exceeded the slight rises in the cost of living index since 1957. With the exception of 1959, rises in nominal wage rates in manufacturing industry have exceeded the annual rise in the cost of living index, and therefore, resulted in a rise in real wages. The substantial increase in money wages was, however, accompanied by significant rises in productivity, especially in the years prior to 1960, and as a consequence inflationary pressures were kept in check.

Business profits

Although the lack of reliable data on profits excludes a thorough analysis of their role in the inflationary process of the 1950's, some observations can be made on the basis of market conditions prevailing at the time.

Throughout the postwar period and until 1953, when imports were liberalized, prevailing conditions in the domestic market provided some justification for the view that opportunities existed for businessmen to realize excessive profit margins. This hypothesis was plausible, in view of the strong demand for consumer goods and the import controls in force, which created a "sellers' market." It is also reasonable to assume that these conditions allowed businessmen to pass on any rise in labor costs to the consumer and maintain their profit margins. Thus, profits appear to have participated actively in the wage price spiral.

The liberalization of imports in 1953 created more competitive conditions in the domestic market. This development, in conjunction with the gradual reduction of excess demand, curtailed the ability of businessmen to enjoy high profit margins. This hypothesis seems to be confirmed, especially since 1956, by available indicators related to industrial profits (see Diagram 8).

On the basis of these indicators, it appears that between 1956 and 1963 profits per unit of output have fallen as a

148

result of increased costs and relatively stable selling prices. Further analysis shows that labor costs increased by 40 per cent, while raw material and fuel costs rose by about 1.5 per cent. Total profits, however, must have risen considerably as a result of a 55 per cent increase in manufacturing output between 1956 and 1963.

DIAGRAM 8

Indices of manufacturing industry

1956=100

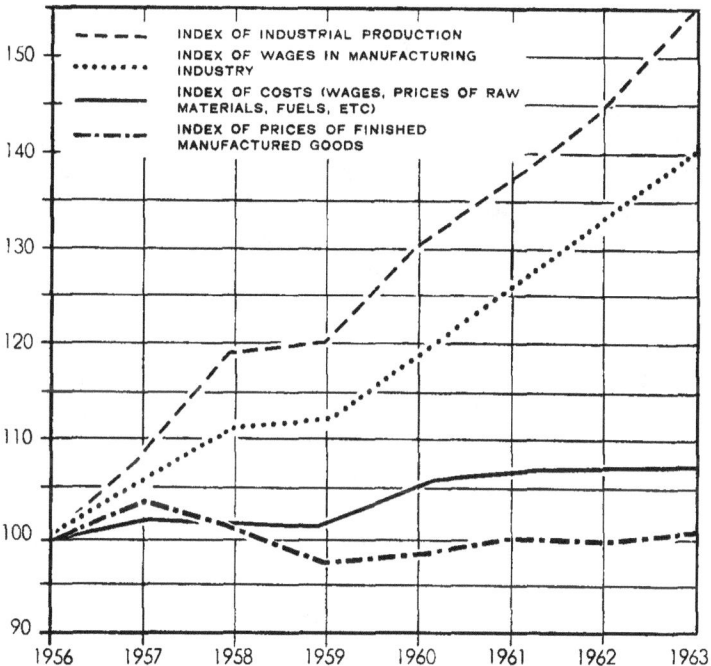

The above indicators seem to lead to the conclusion that, after 1953, foreign competition restricted the ability of businessmen to maintain their profit margins unchanged by passing on increases in costs. Higher profits were now sought through the application of modern technological

149

and organizational methods to production in order to increase productivity.

It would be extremely interesting for policymakers if a study could be made of the subsequent utilization of profits, but available data are not sufficiently reliable for any definite conclusions to be drawn from them. On the basis of existing information, it would appear that a substantial part of business profits has been devoted to luxury consumption.

Price-support policies to agriculture

Throughout the postwar period the authorities have pursued a policy of agricultural price support in order to secure a stable rise in agricultural incomes. In certain cases, however, state intervention in agriculture was aimed at achieving crop readjustment. Agricultural protection was extended on a substantial scale before 1953 in order to compensate for losses in real income inflicted by severe inflation and difficulties in exporting agricultural products.

Agricultural policy affected the inflationary process of the period in three ways. First, it increased the prices of agricultural products consumed mostly by the lower income groups and strengthened their claims for wage increases. Second, to the extent that the cost of the price-support program was not fully covered from sales to domestic consumption, the budget bore the main burden of agricultural support policies. In consequence, the budget deficit increased and added to inflationary pressures. Third, support prices were too often set at levels which virtually excluded Greek products from foreign markets.

The 1953 devaluation of the drachma created favorable conditions for Greek exports and enabled a certain flexibility in agricultural support policies which was maintained until the favorable effects of the devaluation had been largely exhausted. Since 1956, the policies followed have not differed substantially from those of the pre-1953 period.

150

In the long run the real income of the agricultural sector cannot expand indefinitely through a system of supports.

DIAGRAM 9

Percentage changes in agricultural output prices and imports of foodstuffs (one year lag of imports and prices)

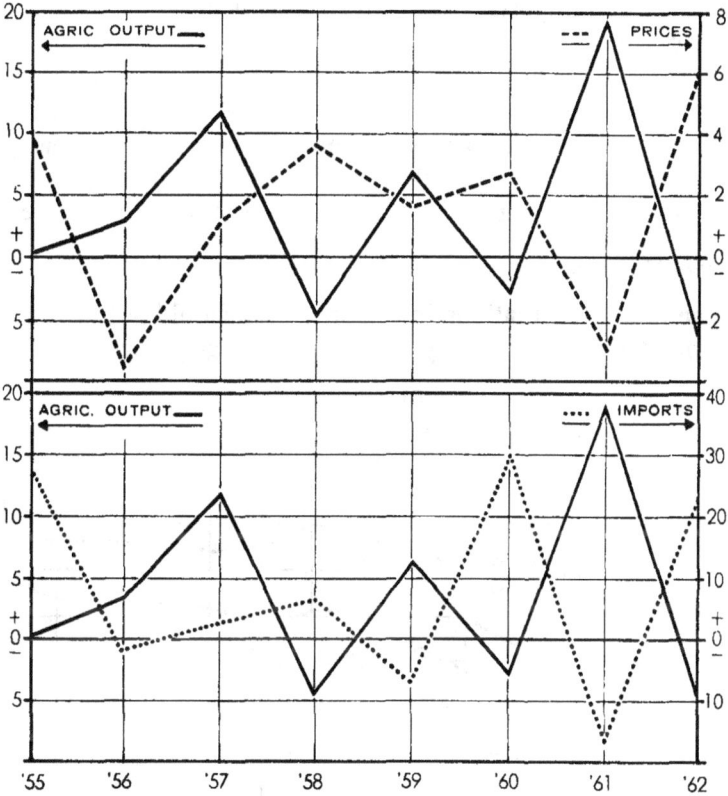

Policy should aim instead at creating conditions which will allow production and distribution costs to be lowered with a consequent rise in net revenue. Price support policies need then only be employed to bring about the necessary changes in crop production in favor of dynamic export products.

Apart from the inflationary impact of agricultural protection policies, the agricultural sector exerted a considerable influence on prices through fluctuations in aggregate production. In periods of bad harvest, the decrease in the supply of agricultural products consumed by the home market resulted in an increase in the consumer price index and in food imports. These effects usually appeared with a lag of one year.

It should be pointed out that though fluctuations in agricultural production in theory should have only a transient and reversible effect on prices, in practice they have a lasting upward influence owing to the tendency of agricultural prices to fall by less than their original rise during a period of bad harvest.

Import prices

The role of fluctuations in import prices should not be underestimated in an economy that is very largely dependent on

DIAGRAM 10

General index of wholesale prices and index of wholesale prices of imported goods

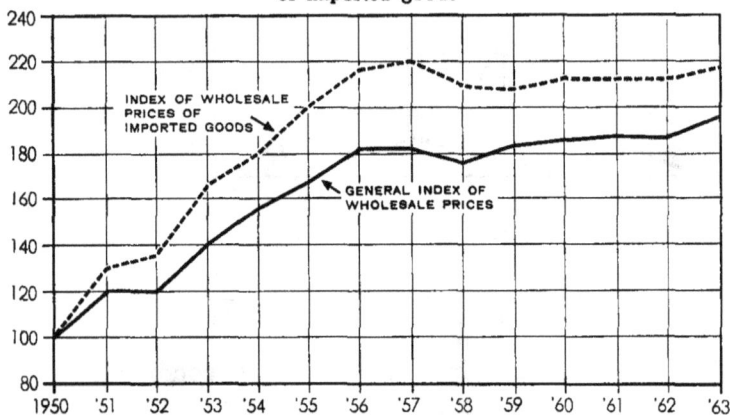

foreign trade. Experience has shown that rises in the prices of imported goods have always been followed by substantial rises in the domestic price level and have led to claims for higher wages.

152

PART TWO

PROBLEMS AND PROSPECTS
OF ECONOMIC DEVELOPMENT

VI

THE HUMAN FACTOR AND THE PROBLEM

OF UNDERDEVELOPMENT [1]

INTRODUCTION

Per capita income is the established criterion for measuring the degree of a country's development. However, the limited usefulness of per capita income as an indicator of economic development often requires that it be supplemented by a series of other indicators and data, such as the structure of production, capital per head, changes in productivity, demographic data, etc., which distinguish the different stages of economic development. In fact there are countries that have long been regarded as advanced industrial nations, although their per capita income would seem to place them among the less-developed—Japan being a case in point. Equally, quite a few West European countries—West Germany is a leading example—experienced a tremendous drop in their national income levels during the war and the early postwar years, but have never been thought of as underdeveloped. Thus, the concept of underdevelopment is significant from the standpoint of economic analysis when it refers, not merely to a given level of per capita income, but to the weaknesses and delays involved in breaking through the "grip of poverty" as the permanent characteristic of an economy. However, no attempt will be made

[1] For a more detailed analysis of many of the topics discussed in the present section see the following studies by the same author, which have been published in the *Papers and Lectures* series of the Bank of Greece: Monetary Stability and Economic Development, 1958; Economic Development and Technical Education, 1960; Regional Planning and Economic Development, 1961; Economic Development and Private Enterprise, 1962; The Role of the Banks in a Developing Country, 1963.

155

here to replace the per capita income criterion by another, for any one quantitative criterion is bound to present similar disadvantages. The position taken here is that it would be possible to make a more realistic approach to the various aspects of the economic development problem and to draw constructive conclusions as to policy objectives and priorities by using a qualitative standard of judgment as an over-all criterion for evaluating growth levels and appraising the results obtained, in addition to the other quantitative criteria that are called for in specific cases. In our opinion, past experience of the relationship between effort and result, aims and accomplishments, tends to show that this criterion should be defined as the quality standard of the contribution made by the human factor to the economic process in terms of technical, organizational and enterpreneurial ability and evolutionary dynamism.

The role of the human factor in the development process has already been stressed in the literature. But the main emphasis has so far been given to the shortage of "dynamic" entrepreneurs. The weaknesses of the human factor have been considered rather as an exogenous restrictive influence of a sociopolitical nature, than as endogenous elements determining the productive utilization of resources.

VARIOUS ASPECTS OF THE PROBLEM

Entrepreneurial underdevelopment

Since the time when Schumpeter made his fundamental contribution to the theory of economic development, the strategic role of the dynamic businessman, introducing novel goods or original production methods and thus opening new vistas for economic activity and development, has been regarded as the force underlying the take off stage of today's advanced economies and as the mainstay of their economic progress. Characteristically, those who have at times expressed the fear that mature economies tend to "stagnate," have found support for their views in the gradual disappearance of the dynamic entrepreneur under the influence of conditions associated with economic maturity and the evolution of sociopolitical concepts and institutions. This anxiety may or may not have been well-founded. In point of fact, since the time when it was expressed, economic growth in the advanced countries has been continuous. Irrespective, however, of the fact that organized collective efforts are playing an increasingly important part in the endeavor to apply modern technology to the production process, there is no doubt that dynamic businessmen have made an enormous contribution to the development of the economically advanced countries.

The foregoing discussion explains why the economic lag of the underdeveloped countries is often attributed to a shortage of this type of creative entrepreneurial dynamism. Although this view is correct in stressing the importance to the economic process of the quality of businessmen, it is not a realistic conception of the entire problem, since it focusses on a single aspect. As a guiding line, therefore, of economic development policy, it leads almost to an impasse, since there are very few, if any, *ad hoc* measures that can directly and rapidly promote the emergence of the ideal type of businessman.

This is not, however, the problem faced by the less developed economies of our age. Nowadays, economic development need not be the outcome of innovations introduced by brilliant pioneers in the field of business and of bold personal initiative in utilizing technological progress, as was the case at the time when today's highly industrialized countries began their development.

Today, the underdeveloped nations of the world have at their disposal a huge and constantly expanding stock of technical know-how and practical expertise. This implies that their development does not necessarily depend on the existence of dynamic innovators capable of breaking new

157

ground. When discussing "economic innovations," we should remember that private initiative in the developing countries is now faced with different conditions from those which prevailed in advanced economies at the time when the pioneers of economic progress first began their activities. Although the transplantation of modern technology and production methods from the mature economies to the underdeveloped countries requires that the latter should effect certain adjustments, creative emulation is definitely an easier task than breaking through the grip of tradition and introducing original methods and products. Emulation does not call for "pioneers" in business but simply requires entrepreneurs with up-to-date training and mentality, a sufficiently broad outlook, and the ability to take advantage of growth potential and business opportunities. In the main, businessmen in developing economies should have the capacity to exercize an effective coordinating function in the production process. It is therefore necessary that entrepreneurs should accept their social responsibilities and acquire the conviction that their own long-term interests, social and economic, are not in conflict with the over-all socioeconomic goals of development.

The problem of entrepreneurial underdevelopment necessitates an improvement in the quality of private enterprise, which must be in a position to face successfully the risks involved in expanding into new sectors, in creative emulation of comparable accomplishments in industrial nations. Experience shows that businessmen in many low-income countries can be both bold and resourceful. But these virtues are either latent or directed towards activities that are undesirable from the standpoint of economic development. The ability of businessmen in underdeveloped regions to carry on systematic and imaginative activities is shown by their initiative in marketing new products—mainly imported commodities—in devising ways and means to increase over-all consumption and in a variety of other profitable ventures. In this connec-

158

tion, it should be mentioned that the international demonstration effect, which strongly influences consumption patterns in underdeveloped countries, has only had a relatively limited influence on production methods and the intensification of the production effort. The strong influence exercized on consumption by the international demonstration effect encourages businessmen to focus their efforts on supplying consumers with new—mostly imported—goods. There has also been a certain influence on production in the sense that it has assisted recognition of the value of modern production methods and mitigated opposition to their introduction in underdeveloped economies. Opposition and obstacles of this kind are directly connected with entrepreneurial underdevelopment and also with the organizational and professional underdevelopment that characterize the economic behavior of the human factor in underdeveloped countries.

Organizational underdevelopment

The low standard of organization in underdeveloped countries is a major feature of their socioeconomic set-up in both the private and—possibly—even more in the public sector. This weakness is reflected in the inability of productive units and government services to function efficiently. Organizational underdevelopment is evident at every level of the organization pyramid. In consequence, efforts to improve the standard of organizational leadership alone are usually of limited effect.

The restrictive influence of organizational underdevelopment on economic progress is obvious. In the private sector, the conception of an original idea and the decision to translate it into action presume a minimum standard of rationality in the existing organization of the enterprises in question. A parallel condition, however, is that the entrepreneur should be convinced that his relations with government agencies and the operation of administrative

159

procedures will promote his plans rather than hold back their realization.

In the public sector, on the other hand, organizational underdevelopment is manifested in the quality of the government's direct contribution to the development effort through the creation of an adequate economic infrastructure, and in the over-all operation of the government machine. Organizational weaknesses in the public sector have a further adverse effect in that they hamper the task of controlling and guiding the private sector in its efforts towards economic growth.

Recognition of the fact that the organizational under-development of the human factor is a common characteristic in both the private and the public sector of less-developed economies should dissolve the myth that the state is all powerful in solving the problems of economic growth. The endeavor to determine *a priori* the optimum degree of expansion of the public sector within the economic devel-opment process cannot lead to a positive conclusion, since the fields of activity of private enterprise and government are determined in practice by the comparative standard of quality of the civil service and of the ability displayed by private enterprise.

Professional underdevelopment

Professional underdevelopment refers to the low standard of knowledge, experience, and responsibility that often characterize the professional performance of the human factor in less-developed economies. The lack of technical know-how and special training is evident in most professions and has a restrictive influence on both the agricultural and in-dustrial sectors, as well as on the sectors of government and services.

Professional underdevelopment is observed mainly in the lack of skilled labor, which in most cases substantially reduces

160

the economic significance of a factor of production that is relatively abundant in underdeveloped countries. The efficient utilization of unskilled manpower is hampered by the lack of technical know-how in the labor force and the psychological difficulty of adapting it to the intensiveness of modern production methods. This, in turn, reflects a limited capacity for technical self-discipline, due to lack of suitable technical education and expertise. Similar weaknesses are also exhibited by management, where the standard of education and experience is often highly inadequate.

Professional underdevelopment also affects the agricultural population where the lack of knowledge and special training has a greater restrictive effect on the introduction of new crops, modern farming methods, and improvements in the quality of produce than the farmer's innate conservatism and mistrust. As a rule, professional underdevelopment also extends to all the professions found in urban centers in the less-developed economies, where the efficiency and standard of trade activities and services are inferior to those of corresponding activities in advanced countries. Uneconomic use of manpower in these sectors is another contributing factor.

Finally, the training of civil servants is very largely either unsuited to the function they perform, or generally inadequate. In view of the major role of government in the development process, the fact that the civil service is not qualified by training and experience to carry out its task efficiently is an aspect of the economic development problem that is as serious as the weaknesses found in the private sector.

The human factor in development strategy

As can be seen from the foregoing analysis, our position on the problem of economic growth is that the development-oriented dynamism of an economy depends far more on

161

entrepreneurial and organizational ability and the specialized training of personnel, than on the size of material factors of production, (capital, natural wealth, etc.). It is instructive to note the far-reaching effect of the progressive influence exerted on certain economies by immigrants with a high educational standard and specialized knowledge —Israel is a case in point.

Instructive results can also be obtained from recent economic and statistical surveys. They show that long-term increases in the output of advanced economies have been decisively affected by nonmaterial factors grouped under the general classification of "technical progress" or "higher productivity." Various deductions have been made from this fact and all of them stress the primary importance of a qualitative improvement of the human factor in achieving a more efficient use of the material factors of production. It is thus widely recognized that the qualitative improvement of the human factor has been a major force underlying economic growth.

In the light of the foregoing, we believe that the most accurate expression of a country's progress and potential for economic development would be an index of the entrepreneurial, organizational, and professional standards of its people. Although this index is only a theoretical possibility, the recognition of the major role of the human factor in the development process should have a fundamental influence on development strategy.

Thus, the importance given until recently to capital shortage as the only obstacle to economic growth does not appear to provide a sound approach to the problem. Although a heavy shortage of capital is a serious disadvantage for underdeveloped countries, it is largely overshadowed by the even greater scarcity of entrepreneurial and organizational abilities and the lack of specially and technically trained human beings. This scarcity is often reflected in the inability of a less-developed country to absorb total available resources for productive purposes. The existence of this problem of absorption shows that, although an increase in the amounts of capital available to an underdeveloped country is a necessary condition for economic progress, it is not always a sufficient one. This does not imply that the need to increase and mobilize savings should consequently be allotted a secondary position in national development programs, but simply indicates that development strategy should increasingly be focussed on mobilizing and improving the human factor. Strong emphasis has been placed on this point in the foregoing discussion because it appears that development policy has hitherto underestimated the need to influence and improve the human factor. Yet the quality and special characteristics of a country's human factor are obviously of decisive importance in determining the formulation and efficacy of economic policy measures.

The influence of the human factor is evident in every aspect of economic development. In the final analysis, even the relative size of the private and public sectors depends on comparative improvements in the quality standard of private enterprise and government services. As mentioned earlier, the degree of relative monetary stability required on any particular occasion depends essentially on the psychological reactions of the public and their sensitivity to temporary or permanent pressures on the national currency. Thus, depending on the temperament and reactions of the population, the same rate of change in monetary magnitudes may either pass unnoticed or cause considerable and widespread disturbances.

Moreover, the level and structure of financing and the corresponding system of credit controls depend on the willingness and ability of entrepreneurs to invest in top priority economic development projects. In less-developed countries, credit controls largely reflect the reduced capacity of the economy to absorb available resources for productive purposes, the excessive propensity for consumption, and the tendency towards less productive, speculative activities.

Similar considerations hold good with respect to tax policy. The structure and efficiency of the tax system depend on the population's attitude towards taxation and on the organization and training of the personnel engaged in tax assessment and collection. When business profits are spent largely on luxuries or are used to finance nonproductive activities, instead of being reinvested in the production process, tax rates should be raised in order to serve socio-political objectives and accelerate economic development. On the contrary, if profits are the main source of financing for the expansion of private productive activities, it would not be wise to turn taxation into a factor that discourages and restricts these activities. Thus, the more complex tasks of fiscal policy are greatly affected by the quality of the human factor.

The human factor also has a substantial effect on the trade, income, and agricultural policies of underdeveloped countries. This influence is reflected in the organization and special training of the agencies and personnel involved, and in the mentality and behavior of the individuals and social groups affected by policy measures.

The foregoing discussion is intended to illustrate the importance of entrepreneurial, organizational, and professional development as a major aim of economic policy. Naturally, the proper orientation of development policy requires a systematic and detailed study of the various aspects and phases of the problem. On broad lines, efforts could focus to advantage on the objectives and activities described below.

SUGGESTED SOLUTIONS

Systematic mobilization of the human factor

The effectiveness of the contribution of the human factor to the economic development effort depends directly on the extent to which it is generally recognized that a sustained process of development is the only way to achieve a lasting improvement in living standards. The initial conversion of public psychology and mentality in favor of economic progress—a change of crucial importance—requires that the concept of economic development be raised to the level of a sociopolitical ideal. The willingness of businessmen, workers, farmers, civil servants, etc., to increase their efforts and assume greater responsibility in their productive activities and their attitude as consumers, depends on their faith in the sound conception and responsible implementation of development programs and on the conviction that they are enjoying an equitable share of the higher national income that they are helping to create. Needless to say, the role and responsibility of political leaders and economic planners alike, are of tremendous importance in the promotion and realization of these aims.

Extension and improvement of education and specialized training

One of the most productive forms of investment is perhaps that which aims at expanding and improving the over-all educational standards of the population. Yet, the share of national income allocated to education in the under-developed countries is wholly inadequate. Moreover, the type of education provided is often irrelevant to actual requirements and does not contribute to the adoption of attitudes conducive to economic development. Thus, the modernization of educational facilities and curricula and the provision of free and compulsory education to all children of school age would provide a valuable form of development-promoting infrastructure.

At the same time, it is necessary to improve the standard of vocational education and training in the light of present-day employment requirements.

An improvement in the quality of entrepreneurship can

165

be obtained through a coordinated special training program. The main problem is the provision of the necessary schools to train executives in modern practices and advanced methods of business administration. These schools should have a business-oriented approach to their subject in order to facilitate a sound appreciation of the problem of maximizing business profits within the framework of economic development, a rational exploitation of opportunities for expanding productive activities in the long run and, generally, a widening in the economic horizons of new entrepreneurs. The curricula and methods of operation of these schools require detailed study. Close cooperation between advanced and developing countries in this field is of fundamental importance.

It is also imperative to introduce more systematic and comprehensive training for civil servants, which is a basic prerequisite for improving the efficiency of the government machine in its ordinary current functions and in its direct participation in the development process. This objective necessitates the establishment of special schools, which will not only provide knowledge and instruction but cultivate a sense of responsibility and the capacity for creative initiative in carrying out the tasks of a civil servant.

Labor training and specialization programs should be given absolute priority in development policy. This is essential in order to improve and modernize the technical standards of the labor force and to satisfy the sociopolitical necessities of an effective solution to the acute problems of unemployment and underemployment. Experience has shown that unemployment and underemployment are found chiefly in the unskilled portion of the labor force, while skilled manpower is more readily absorbed at every stage of economic development.

The glaring disproportion between the very limited supply of skilled labor and the excessive supply of unskilled manpower, as well as the generally very low standard of

166

training and specialization in the labor force of underdeveloped countries, would perhaps justify the view that, in these countries, skilled labor is as scarce as capital, if not more so. Although it is usually argued that unemployment and underemployment in less-developed economies are both due to the scarcity of complementary factors of production (capital in particular), it would nevertheless be difficult to answer the question whether unemployed—and as a rule, unskilled—labor in these economies can become, in its present form, a complementary factor to capital in modern production processes and at acceptable cost levels. Skilled labor shortages in the less-developed economies—though differing in degree of intensity according to the stage of development and the cultural level of each country—cause very serious bottlenecks in the development process. Within the general context of each country's conditions, available capital is often faced with a complete lack of suitable labor or with qualitatively inadequate manpower. Thus, the lack of skilled labor has as strong a restrictive influence on the inflow of foreign private capital into the underdeveloped countries as that exercized by the lack of infrastructure and external economies.

Clearly, it is essential to make an intensive and systematic effort to raise the standard of technical education and training. This is one way of creating capital, human capital, and is of top economic priority, as well as being desirable from the social standpoint. The effort should be made on a broad basis covering the entire population and should include the establishment of adequate numbers of technical schools on a long-term basis and the introduction of special intensive training and specialization programs for the labor force in general.

Institutional and organizational improvements

The institutional environment in any given country is essentially the outcome of historical developments and reflects the over-all cultural standard it has attained. In principle, therefore, there are limited possibilities for radically changing existing institutions by introducing economic and general policy measures better adjusted to the aims of economic development. Nevertheless, to the extent that the population is aware of the need for economic development, there are considerable margins for institutional and organizational improvements intended to facilitate the best possible mobilization of the human factor.

Particular importance should be attached to the improvement of the system of financial rewards and penalties, to make it better adapted to the individual's success or failure in his activities. This holds true for both entrepreneurs and government and private employees. The continued existence of nonviable productive units or branches through government assistance is definitely restrictive to economic progress. Equally restrictive is the discouraging tax and credit treatment of economically successful businessmen. Moreover, the private and public sectors in less-developed countries are characterized by inadequate wage differentiation on the basis of the above criteria, and by the limited importance attached to ability in professional advancement —both among private employees and civil servants. This combination is a serious counter-incentive in the mobilization and improvement of the human factor. The need for rapid economic development and the strategic role of the human factor necessitates that in underdeveloped countries—perhaps even more than in advanced economies—pecuniary and nonpecuniary rewards should be scaled in direct relation to the abilities of individuals.

In developing economies, it is necessary to control and regulate monopolies. The privileged position of monopolists naturally encourages them to aim at maintaining the *status quo* under which, through market-sharing agreements and other practices they avoid the intensification of their efforts that would be essential if they faced competition. Therefore, the proper mobilization of entrepreneurial and professional potential in underdeveloped countries requires that conditions of competitive effort and initiative should be established in every sector of productive activity through the gradual elimination, *inter alia,* of the institution of "closed trades," which is wholly incompatible with the needs of a developing economy.

In many less-developed countries there are social groups or economic sectors which, compared with other groups or sectors, display greater capabilities or are better organized for undertaking productive initiatives. The opportunities provided by such a differentiation should be suitably utilized, possibly by expanding relevant activities beyond the traditional sphere of operation found in mature economies. This is especially advocated with respect to the banking system, which has great responsibilities in the developing countries and is normally better organized than other sectors of the economy. In such countries the banks have the important duty of effecting an optimal distribution of credit among the various sectors of the economy, according to economic development priorities. As far as possible, this should be left to the initiative and discretion of private banks, independent of intervention by the monetary authorities, since, in the last analysis, economic development serves the long-term interests of the banks in the best possible way. Apart from this, however, the banking system can encourage and stimulate private initiative by expanding its activities into the field of technical services of interest to businessmen, facilitating their communication with foreign entrepreneurs and banks, and participating directly in the equity capital of new or expanding firms. The utilization of part of the availabilities of commercial banks in order to finance capital formation, mainly in industry, although an unorthodox practice, is particularly advisable in many cases. In the less advanced economies, the banks have a long-standing tradition and great prestige, and generally enjoy the public's confidence. It is, therefore, easier for them to mobilize private savings than it is for private entrepreneurs.

It could be argued in this context that the nature and structure of commercial bank deposits does not provide a suitable basis for the long-term financing of industry. In each case, however, this is a question of assessing actual conditions in particular countries. In Greece for instance, an increase in long-term deposits with the commercial banks, in conjunction with the possibility of drawing long-term capital by selling securities or borrowing from abroad, can ensure the liquidity of the banks and enhance their solvency. Furthermore, the banks can be assisted in carrying out their task by the provision of central bank funds and facilities for discounting their medium and long-term portfolios under certain conditions. Finally, the banks' contribution towards expanding the industrial sector can be increased by the participation of government funds channeled through the banking system.

VII

PROSPECTS AND PROBLEMS

IN GREEK ECONOMIC DEVELOPMENT

INTRODUCTION

During the past fifteen years the Greek economy has made substantial progress which will be of decisive importance for the country's future.

The Greek economy has now reached a turning point. Developments in the next decade will show whether Greece will be able to break the grip of underdevelopment and raise her national income to the level of an economically advanced nation. Future needs are numerous and require undivided attention. Greece must not fail to profit by past experience, which can be of valuable assistance in avoiding unnecessary mistakes and improving the national effort. In this context the following points are of basic importance:

First, securing' monetary equilibrium in the Greek economy has laid the foundations of the country's economic development and is an indispensable condition to further economic progress. Monetary equilibrium has been established on a firm ground and experience shows that it can successfully withstand strong pressures. Under these conditions the maintenance of a healthy monetary environment should not exert any unduly limiting influence on the pursuit of a policy aiming at rapid development.

Second, the 'progress achieved hitherto in the country's economy is attributable mainly to an expansion of productive capacity, with limited improvements in the structure of production. This is evident both in the small changes in the relative shares of primary, secondary, and tertiary production in the national product and in the absence of radical

171

improvements in the composition of sectoral outputs. It is true that agriculture and manufacturing are supplying new products many of which are suitable for export, and the tourist trade has gained particular importance in the sector of services. However, the annual fluctuations in the growth rate of the Greek economy show that it is still heavily dependent on weather and other natural conditions affecting agricultural output. One of the main symptoms which indicate the weaknesses inherent in the country's economy is the relative stagnation in exports and the lack of substantial improvement in their composition.

Third, there have been several weaknesses in planning economic development in Greece. Since the rate of economic growth is substantially influenced by the existence of a complete and properly implemented development program, it is necessary to improve economic planning rapidly and effectively, as discussed in further detail below.

Fourth, the main factors retarding economic development are attributable to weaknesses of the human factor and to unfavorable conditions for a fuller utilization of capabilities. We believe this point to be of vital importance as it has a crucial influence on the country's economic development. The shortage of capital and the general inadequacy of factors of production and natural resources bear less responsibility for the delays observed in the process of economic growth, than the weaknesses and deficiencies of the human factor, both in the private and the public sector. It should be stressed, however, that the Greek people if properly trained and motivated, possess the inherent qualities needed to achieve a faster rate of development.

THE CONCEPT AND ROLE OF PLANNING IN ECONOMIC DEVELOPMENT

Weaknesses in economic planning are not peculiar to Greece alone. Similar weaknesses have been observed to a greater or

172

lesser degree in most of the development plans of other less-developed countries. In our opinion, this is mainly due to the special difficulties of economic planning and the implementation of development plans in free-enterprise economies.

In a free-enterprise economy which relies on private ownership of the means of production and on the market mechanism, economic development is basically dependent on private initiative. The state is assumed to limit its role to the creation of economic infrastructure and the introduction of certain measures to influence the market mechanism in desirable directions, according to specific economic policy objectives. However, if the state restricts itself to these activities, it will prove difficult to accelerate economic progress. Systematic economic planning is, therefore, a necessity. Today, planning is generally acknowledged to be an indispensable factor in the progress of underdeveloped countries towards the level of economic development attained by other countries in the 19th century through private initiative alone. The formulation of a long-term development plan to exploit natural resources and to utilize available manpower is the first step toward the implementation of a constructive economic development policy. Such a plan determines : (1) a desirable rate of growth, which is consistent with the preservation of internal and external monetary equilibrium; (2) the spheres of activity of government and private enterprise in the development process; (3) the organization of the distribution of productive resources between consumption and investment; and (4) the best procedure for guiding private initiative in the desired directions.

The plan should also indicate the policy to be adopted if private initiative proves incapable of achieving the targets set for the private sector despite the offered incentives and other measures of support.

Needless to say, the part to be played by the state within the framework of a free enterprise economy cannot

173

be strictly defined. The distribution of activities between the public and private sector does not take place on the basis of theoretical criteria. It depends on actual social and economic conditions, the standard of managerial ability, and especially the degree of development of private entrepreneurial activity. On broad lines, however, the dividing line between the role of government and that of private initiative is determined on the following basis: Government undertakes the tasks of formulating the over-all economic development program, carrying out economic infrastructure projects, including the vital sector of technical and vocational training, and guiding private economic activity through its credit, fiscal, and trade policy toward the realization of the objectives of the program. Private initiative, on the other hand, normally covers all other activities involved in economic development. The direct participation of government in productive activity and investment is usually rather limited, except in the previously mentioned case of economic infrastructure.

Obviously, the formulation and implementation of a development plan in a free economy inevitably include more unknown factors and are far less amenable to arbitrary policy criteria than in centrally planned economies. In a planned economy, profit maximization does not constitute the basic factor in planning. Consumer freedom is substantially restricted, and the foreign sector is controlled. These factors, however, are among the most dynamic features of a free-enterprise economy. In conjunction with the free operation of private enterprise, they constitute certain aspects of economic development planning that are not encountered in planned economies. In consequence, the planning techniques of free economies differ from those applied in centrally planned economies. On the whole, they are more complicated, since they have to formulate policies that can influence a multitude of economic magnitudes and trends.

It is not intended to deal with planning techniques in

174

the present chapter. Excellent studies have already been published on this subject—especially under the auspices of the United Nations. The foregoing discussion attempts mainly to stress that the success of even the most perfect technique depends on a realistic approach to its application. It is therefore appropriate to discuss in further detail a number of specific problems related to the formulation and implementation of the Greek economic development program in the light of past experience and of existing conditions in the Greek economy.

Problems Connected with the Compilation of the Economic Development Program

The Greek economy is now entering a phase of development in which economic planning is of crucial importance and the improvement of methodology is a vital need.

Economic planning should be based on modern scientific methods and should take full advantage of the possibilities they offer for accelerating the rate of economic development. In turn, this depends on the proper training and specialization of the staff involved in the preparation of the program. Improved planning techniques are also necessary in order to convince the public that the efforts that they are called on to make will have effective results. As already emphasized, public confidence is essential if a sense of cooperation toward a common purpose is to be engendered. Moreover, the provision of financial and other forms of aid from advanced countries and international organizations depends increasingly on the existence of satisfactory programs covering the whole economy as well as individual development projects.

Since economic development is a complex process, the successful formulation of the development program requires a clear outline of objectives and setting of priorities. Although the final evaluation of development goals depends on the

175

judgement of political leaders, economic planners should determine existing possibilities and carry out detailed analyses to decide whether the various targets are complementary or conflicting. In this way, the problem of choosing among different methods will be clarified and the best combination of economic policy measures appropriate to each case will be resolved. The essence of economic planning consists in the strategic choice and establishment of priorities for individual development targets.

For a successful choice of immediate aims for development policy, it is essential to look at the problems from a long-term aspect. Long-term considerations often change the substance of economic problems. When problems and development potentialities are regarded in the light of long-run prospects, they frequently lead to wholly different conclusions and policies from those dictated by the short-term considerations of the same problems and conditions. Indeed, the most serious structural problems in economic development can be properly conceived and solved only if considered in the context of long-term trends and prospects. It is therefore advisable to lay down a fairly long-term program which will incorporate the "five-year" development plans of the Greek economy. This will ensure a sounder evaluation of individual problems and facilitate a more effective stage-by-stage revision of short-term plans during their implementation, according to current conditions.

A systematic analysis of characteristic and strategic parameters in the Greek economy is an indispensable condition to the adoption of modern planning methods and the accurate evaluation of the country's problems and possibilities for development. When the interdependence and quantitative aspects of crucial economic problems remain unknown, development planning necessarily contains substantial gaps and serious defects. Such knowledge is indispensable to a coherent policy of government intervention and to a safer and consistent forecast of prospective developments in indi-

176

vidual economic sectors. The availability of this analytical and statistical material is an essential foundation for modern economic planning.

It will therefore be necessary to carry out a series of econometric and other studies, which will allow a more accurate evaluation of the present structure and future prospects of the Greek economy.

A series of detailed technical and economic studies for the implementation of special programs and projects of strategic importance to the development of individual sectors and areas of the country's economy must also be compiled.

PROBLEMS ARISING FROM THE IMPLEMENTATION OF AN ECONOMIC DEVELOPMENT PROGRAM

The past experience of underdeveloped countries suggests two basic conclusions regarding the agencies involved in the implementation of economic development plans: in the first place, private initiative in the less-developed econo-mies is not always capable by itself of promoting econom-ic development satisfactorily, owing to the relative lack of entrepreneurial abilities, organizational talent, and tech-nical know-how. Secondly, it is impossible for government in a free enterprise developing economy to replace successfully private initiative on a large scale since the public sector suffers from the same weaknesses as its private counterpart. On the other hand, foreign private initiative, which possesses the required abilities to develop entrepreneurial activities does not show sufficient willingness to play this role in the less-developed countries. When it does, it is often not prop-erly adapted to the development requirements of these regions.

The problem of the private sector therefore has three aspects: First, how to mobilize domestic private initiative in a less advanced economy and enable it to operate successfully under internationally competitive conditions. Second, how to attract foreign private enterprise towards productive activities in a developing country. And third, how to secure constructive cooperation between foreign and domestic enterprises.

The mere provision of incentives and other economic policy measures has already proved inadequate and another approach becomes necessary. In countries which have attained a certain degree of development, such as many Latin American countries or Greece, it will be easier to find a solution to the problem within the framework of a free enterprise economy if government makes a more systematic effort to mobilize private initiative. Under the free enterprise system it would not, of course, be conceivable for government intervention to reach the point of nationalizing the major part of the industrial sector. In fact, it is questionable whether it would be feasible for the governments of underdeveloped countries to intervene directly in productive activity on a very wide scale.

Cooperation between the advanced countries and countries seeking faster economic development would enable the latter to formulate a system for mobilizing their private sectors and a self-sustained development process would gradually evolve. The first step would be for the government of each developing country to take the initiative in establishing a special organization intended exclusively for promoting private entrepreneurial activity. Organizations of this kind have already been set up in several countries, but this is not enough. The inadequacy of technical know-how and organizational ability in the less-developed countries affects the government machine and its weaknesses are reflected in the agencies in question. The efforts of such an agency would not suffice to neutralize the effects of all the factors that exert a restrictive influence on the flow of foreign capital and enterprise towards investment and productive activities in less-developed countries. The advanced nations should, there-

178

fore, assist the underdeveloped countries by creating organizations in their own countries which would endeavor to mobilize domestic enterprise to undertake productive activities in less-advanced economies.

Industrial development organizations in the less advanced countries should be independent bodies in the form of corporations with government participation in their equity capital and should be entrusted with the task of paving the way for industrial investment by undertaking the necessary technical studies. They should also endeavor to set up new enterprises or participate in the share capital of private industrial concerns and organize a system for the provision of consulting services and technical and managerial personnel to interested firms. By projecting industrial investment opportunities, undertaking technical studies, and securing the cooperation of foreign enterprise and capital, these organizations would offset the inadequacy of entrepreneurial initiative in underdeveloped countries and help to raise the standard of technical and organizational ability by providing technical advice and training for high-level personnel. Corresponding organizations should be established in the advanced countries to act in cooperation with their counterparts in the developing economies, with the joint aim of promoting the flow of capital and business initiative to the underdeveloped regions of the world. These organizations should collaborate closely with the respective bodies in the developing countries to obtain information concerning investment opportunities and should undertake the promotion of suitable investment schemes within the business community of their own country. Further, these organizations could greatly facilitate the task of domestic industrial development organizations in the field of technical studies and the provision of qualified administrative and technical staff. The proposed system should be governed by the following basic principles:

First, since the main aim of the system is the promotion

179

of private investment and productive activity, and not the replacement of private initiative by public investment, the earliest possible transfer of newly established firms to the private sector is a basic condition for the fulfilment of the objectives of the system.

Second, the criteria that industrial development organizations will use as a basis for selecting the various sectors of economic activity and the establishment of new firms should be business-oriented, to allow for the ultimate transfer of the new firms to private business.

Third, as mentioned earlier, the successful promotion of private initiative and enterprise requires that newly established production units should be profit minded. At the same time, however, if the organizations are to make an effective contribution to economic development, they must select and place productive schemes in the order of priority dictated by over-all socioeconomic objectives.

Fourth, it is of basic importance that the industrial development organizations should cooperate with the banks in an effort to develop the capital market. The attraction of larger amounts of savings into this market will be greatly facilitated by offering for sale the shares issued by the new, well-organized and efficient units established by the organizations, or stocks from the expansion of the equity capital of existing firms, whose standing will be further enhanced by the organizations' backing. Through the widest possible spread of the shares issued by firms created by the industrial development organizations it would also be possible to enlarge the ownership of share capital.

Fifth, the cooperation of foreign enterprise in the industrialization of developing economies should mainly take the form of joint enterprises, which have the particular advantage of combining the organizational abilities and entrepreneurial experience possessed by business in the industrial nations with the specialized experience and knowledge of local conditions available to domestic businessmen.

THE HUMAN FACTOR IN THE DEVELOPMENT OF THE GREEK ECONOMY

The importance of the contribution of the human factor to economic development was discussed at considerable length in the preceding chapter. We shall now examine some points that are of special significance to actual conditions in Greece.

In the first place, the general public and the agencies involved in development planning and implementation should become fully aware of the fact that economic development is based on the active participation of the entire population, which should be ready and willing to make greater efforts and accept temporary sacrifices. In this sense, a developing economy is in some ways similar to a wartime economy. The concept of economic development should thus be raised to the level of a socioeconomic ideal. It will also be the task of political leaders to make the people understand that economic development does not necessarily imply sacrificing the present generation for the benefit of the next. On the contrary, by diverting part of the potential rise in consumption to current savings and investment it will be possible to increase consumption fairly rapidly to a level that would have been wholly unattainable without increasing investment. The truth is that economic growth can benefit both present and future generations. However, the fair distribution of sacrifices and benefits between successive generations requires judicious evaluation by political leaders. In democratic countries political leaders are controlled by the people, who must therefore be given the appropriate guidance.

Even more important than the intertemporal distribution of economic development benefits is their sharing among

181

the different classes of the population on a more equitable basis. The degree of inequality in income distribution and the level of economic development are inversely related. Disregard for social justice in income distribution is a rather typical characteristic of underdevelopment and further intensifies it. All attempts at economic development will be devoid of content and prone to failure if they are aimed at serving sectional interests at the expense of the wider masses of the population.

Education, the specialization of workers and farmers, the technical and professional training of managerial and administrative staff are top priority investments. Moreover, as these investments concern the entire population, they gradually reduce the inequality of opportunity for personal progress and serve both social justice and the aims of development by bringing those with the greatest talent to the fore.

The reorganization of the various branches and levels of the country's educational system is a complex problem which requires further research and analysis. Among the different aspects of this problem, particular importance should be attached to the need for an over-all improvement in the standard of technical experience and training. Technical education and specialization in the industrial countries is as much the outcome of training in special schools as of living in an environment where technical know-how is a tradition even at the family level. Thus, the acquisition of knowledge and experience of a technical nature in the industrial nations is the result of the effective influence exercized on the younger generation by both the educational system and the social environment.

In contrast, the quantitative and qualitative inadequacy of technical education in the underdeveloped countries is further aggravated by the lack of a technological tradition, and the social environment thus contributes very little to the over-all effort to obtain a better educated labor force. So long as industrial development is still in its infancy, the main burden of providing the population with technical knowledge has to be borne by the technical schools. Under these circumstances, an effective improvement in technical education in the underdeveloped countries is obviously a major objective.

Similar considerations hold with respect to the human factor in agriculture, on which we shall dwell in a following chapter.

Institutional and Organizational Improvements

A decisive mobilization of the human factor and the success of the structural changes needed for the development of the Greek economy necessitate the introduction of a number of institutional and organizational improvements.

In this general context, we must stress the decisive importance of securing conditions favorable to the unimpeded operation of the market mechanism. In many cases, the normal functioning of the price mechanism and the private sector in general is distorted and hindered by monopolies and the multitude and irrationality of government interventions. The price mechanism in an underdeveloped economy is, of course, full of imperfections requiring the corrective intervention of the government. But any such intervention must be carried out in a rational manner so as to assist the market mechanism to make a greater contribution to the process of economic development. Government intervention in the Greek economy so far has consisted largely of a variety of unrelated and often incompatible measures, which were initially taken in order to cope with specific situations and have now accumulated into a meaningless whole. Preventive and restrictive controls, special licences, outdated restrictions, and a maze of other regulations have formed a stifling and uncoordinated complex of restrictions, that indirectly increases the costs of private enterprise and impedes or restricts the development

183

of private initiative. The inadequacy of private initiative and enterprise in the Greek economy has already been stressed and is not unrelated to the above-mentioned counter-incentives, the restrictive influences of which should not be underestimated. It is imperative to reformulate government intervention policy on a rational basis and to eliminate the counter-incentives created by it as quickly as possible.

The provision of incentives to the private sector of the Greek economy is another important question, since those provided so far have been of limited effect. It is probable that these incentives were largely neutralized by tax evasion and the counter-incentives mentioned.

Another vitally important question is the reorganization of government services, particularly those controlling and guiding productive activity. It should be generally understood that the role of government officials within the framework of the Greek economy is not limited merely to the traditional functions of the government machine but has a decisive part to play in economic development. The organization and operation of government services, whether as agencies directly involved in economic activity or as bodies guiding and controlling private productive activities, should be radically improved. The whole question is related to the problem of counter-incentives already mentioned and its solution depends essentially on the creation of a psychological climate which is strongly in favor of economic progress.

VIII

THE PROBLEMS OF EMPLOYMENT

AND EMIGRATION

INTRODUCTION

If the human factor is to be effectively mobilized in Greece, decisive measures will be necessary to resolve the problems of employment and emigration. The Greek economy is faced with open or disguised unemployment and underemployment, which impinge mainly on the unskilled—the largest portion of the active population. Unemployment and underemployment constitute a complex economic and social problem, since the unemployed represent not only unutilized productive potential but also human beings living in a climate of rising expectations, yet unable to secure a tolerable standard of living. Even if this state of affairs is somewhat mitigated by subsistence allowances and other social welfare benefits—almost always inadequate despite the socioeconomic burden they entail—the essence of the problem remains the same. A man who is out of work or underemployed does not undergo economic privations alone. He suffers at the same time from morale deterioration and this makes the problem even more urgent and acute.

The attainment of high employment levels is a central objective of economic development programs all over the world and is usually one of the major criteria in determining investment priorities. However, in underdeveloped economies where, under the existing production techniques, a balanced structure of the factors of production is usually lacking, employment maximization does not always coincide with output and income maximization, as it largely does in mature economies. The effort to maximize the labor utilized per unit of investment is likely to lead eventually

185

to deviations from the maximum possible rate of economic development, a fact which is bound to prolong the technological backwardness and low productivity of the underdeveloped countries.

We have already stressed the view that the acceleration of the G.N.P. growth rate should be the main development objective. The realization of this aim will also bring about eventually a satisfactory solution of employment problems. Meanwhile, until this goal is achieved, the question of employment must be actively pursued in the following two directions:

First, an effective policy should be adopted to promote those branches of production, particularly in the industrial sector, that are labor intensive, and satisfy all other essential criteria for receiving priority under economic development programs.

Second, special programs should be set up for the purpose of training unskilled and unemployed workers, who should receive living allowances during their training period. If the rate of unemployment is high, projects should be chiefly designed to mitigate acute unemployment in a particular area or class of the population. Such measures would provide some of the unemployed with a source of livelihood, prevent prolonged idleness from becoming a habitual way of life, and improve the level of expertise and specialization of the labor force.

It is of basic importance that these programs, and social policies in general, should not be confused with economic development policy. The rationality and effectiveness of both require that a clear distinction be drawn between measures aimed at stimulating the development-promoting forces of the economy and those directed mainly at satisfying immediate needs of a sociopolitical nature.

EMPLOYMENT AND EMIGRATION
THE PROBLEM IN GREECE

Unemployment has long been a serious and pressing problem in the Greek economy. Although economic progress so far has helped improve conditions to some extent, it has not solved the problem. In many cases, especially in the sector of secondary production, the increase in output has been achieved mainly through a rise in productivity rather than an increase in employment. There are also clear indications of a considerable degree of underemployment in the sector of services. On the other hand, the movement of the farming population to other employment in the cities or abroad has caused symptoms of labor shortage in some agricultural regions, while other areas are still faced with problems of inadequate employment and seasonal underemployment.

In recent years, population surpluses have been absorbed to a considerable extent by rapidly increasing emigration. In all cases emigration presents itself as an emergency solution. Viewed in the perspective of the next few years in Greece, the disadvantages of extensive emigration outweigh its advantages. The actual and potential benefits to the national economy from emigration may be summarized as follows:

First, the major direct benefit is the inflow of emigrants' remittances, which represent a sizeable source of foreign exchange earnings and substantially supplement the incomes of the poorer population groups, especially in the rural areas. It should be borne in mind, however, that emigrants' remittances are only a part of the earnings of Greek workers abroad and that their productive activities are lost to the national economy. Moreover, the inflow of these remittances will gradually diminish as whole families emigrate and their ties with the homeland become looser in the course of time.

Second, it has been maintained that emigration reduces population pressure on the resources of underdeveloped economies and thereby facilitates the accumulation of savings and the transfer of factors of production from the consumer sector to investment. This may be particularly significant for countries with a very high rate of population growth but does not apply to Greece. Furthermore, increasing savings and utilizing productively any such increase are conditions not easy to realize—especially when emigration absorbs the best trained and most dynamic segment of the active population.

Third, as Table 59 shows, the largest, and constantly increasing portion of the total number of emigrants in the past four years has been directed towards Western European countries. There are good grounds for hoping that emigration to these countries, as opposed to emigration overseas, will not be of a permanent nature and that it will eventually be possible for a considerable number of emigrants to return to Greece and to take an active and decisive part in her national development effort. The experience and skills in modern production techniques acquired by Greek emigrants abroad, particularly those employed in the industrial sector, represent an important investment in "human capital," which can become a major factor in promoting the country's industrialization. If most of the emigrants actually return, then their emigration to Europe will have the beneficial effect of a mass training program for the country's labor force.

However, a turn of the tide, from emigration to repatriation, may not necessarily coincide with favorable prospects at home, such as could result from an acceleration in the rate of Greek economic development offering employment opportunities attractive enough to bring them back. It could simply be the consequence of an economic recession of some duration in Europe. Although there is no immediate likelihood of any such economic disturbance, it remains a possibility which might materialize in the future. Greek workers, who form a marginal portion of the labor force in foreign countries would then be among the first to suffer

TABLE 59

Emigration from Greece, 1955–1963

Years	Total of emigrants	Total of emigrants from industrial labor force	Per cent of total	DESTINATION Overseas countries Total of emigrants	Per cent of total	Western Europe Total of emigrants[a]	Per cent of total	Mediterranean countries Total of emigrants	Per cent of total	Not declared
			2 : 1		4 : 1		6 : 1		8 : 1	
	1	2	3	4	5	6	7	8	9	10
1955	29,787	2,647	8.9	19,772	66.4	6,068	20.4	3,747	12.6	200
1956	35,349	3,154	8.9	23,147	65.5	7,780	22.0	4,181	11.8	241
1957	30,428	2,586	8.5	14,783	48.6	13,046	42.9	2,415	7.9	184
1958	24,521	3,418	13.9	14,842	60.5	6,567	26.8	2,998	12.2	114
1959	23,684	4,209	17.8	13,871	58.6	6,713	28.3	2,696	11.4	404
1960	47,768	17,132	35.9	17,764	37.2	26,927	56.4	2,848	6.0	229
1961	58,837	26,994	45.9	17,336	29.5	39,564	67.2	1,730	2.9	207
1962	84,054	47,267	56.2	21,959	26.1	60,754	72.3	1,141	1.4	200
1963	100,072	54,070	54.0	24,459	24.4	74,236	74.2	1,113	1.1	264

[a] It should be borne in mind that a substantial proportion (20–30% annually) of emigrant workers returns to Greece

Sources: National Statistical Service of Greece, *Statistical Yearbooks 1956–1962, Monthly Statistical Bulletin*, February and March 1964.

the consequences of a recession of some duration. In other words, should employment levels drop, Greek workers would naturally be laid off in favor of their foreign workmates. Thus, Greek emigrants not only contribute their skill and effort towards the progress of foreign economies but also provide a considerable margin of safety for local workers. The return of emigrants, before the necessary conditions for their productive absorption into the Greek economy are established, would create serious problems and could assume the proportions of a flood of refugees into Greece. It is essential, therefore, that the repatriation of Greek workers and the utilization of their acquired skill and experience should be based on faster economic development, which would create employment opportunities more attractive than those offered abroad and would lead to a gradual return of emigrants to Greece from the countries where they are now employed.

The advantages and disadvantages of emigration are related to the magnitude of the migratory movement, its structure, and the economic conditions and prospects obtaining in the country of origin. The adverse effects of emigration on the Greek economy may be summarized as follows:

First, the number of Greek emigrants, which has exceeded the annual population growth in the last three years, rose by a further 19 per cent in 1963 (see Table 59). Emigration may thus evolve from a temporary outlet for surplus population into a factor that will restrict economic development in Greece.

Second, rapid emigration combined with a low and decelerating population growth rate has an adverse effect on the population pyramid and may lead to socioeconomic senility.

Third, as Table 59 shows, the structure of emigration is particularly unfavorable to the Greek economy. The

190

number of emigrants coming from the industrial labor force is gradually rising and exceeded half of the total emigration in both 1962 and 1963.

Moreover, the fact that a large number of Greek students at foreign universities fail to return, deprives the Greek economy of scientific personnel in short supply.

Fourth, the abundance of labor is an important incentive to the establishment of foreign enterprises and production units in Greece. Emigration curtails the effectiveness of this incentive.

Emigration has long been a painful tradition in this country and the inevitable result of underdevelopment. A rapid and effective effort to develop the Greek economy is, therefore, the only course that can ultimately provide a solution to the problem of emigration. In the intervening period, until it becomes possible and generally beneficial for Greek workers to return from abroad, the country's emigration policy should aim chiefly at the following goals:

1. As far as possible, the number of Greek workers abroad should be stabilized by creating a flow of repatriates almost equal in number to new emigrants. Estimates show that the number of Greek workers returning from abroad is very considerable and probably amounts to about one-third of the total number of emigrants in the past three years. It may, therefore, be said that Greek workers are already coming back at a substantial rate, which should be increased further in order to offset emigration to the largest extent possible under present circumstances. As it is neither advisable nor feasible to regulate emigration and repatriation on a compulsory basis, the employment and remuneration conditions necessary to check emigration and attract Greek labor back to the home country can obviously only be attained by accelerating economic development.

A continuous training process will thus be instituted, to the benefit of a considerable portion of the Greek labor force. The emigrant population will be constantly in process of renewal, without increasing in size. To the extent that the Greek economy reaches higher income and employment levels, the ultimate goal of emigration policy should be to increase repatriation and thus effect the return of all Greek workers from abroad. To this end, it would be advisable for the government to undertake a continuous and systematic effort to inform Greek workers living abroad of employment opportunities in Greece. A service should be organized, to collect detailed information on the demand of Greek firms for skilled labor and circulate it to Greek workers living abroad. Many of these workers would be willing to return in certain circumstances, but are prevented from doing so by their ignorance of current conditions in the Greek labor market.

2. Greek workers emigrating to foreign countries should derive the greatest possible benefit from their stay abroad and at the same time maintain close ties with their homeland. The appropriate government services should be more systematically organized and should collaborate with their counterparts in foreign countries to provide Greek emigrants with employment in sectors which offer better specialization and more useful experience. At the same time, the government must take steps to improve the living conditions of Greek workers abroad by giving them guidance and support and providing all possible assistance for them to maintain strong links with their country.

IX

PROBLEMS AND PROSPECTS IN GREEK INDUSTRIAL DEVELOPMENT[1]

THE NEED FOR INDUSTRIALIZATION IN GREECE

As a rule industrial expansion is a major objective in low-income countries since they consider it a basic condition for the success of their over-all economic development efforts.

Although, in theory, economic development can be realized without industry being the leading sector, in actual practice this is fairly difficult if not impossible to achieve, unless there are especially favorable conditions for expanding production and exports of primary products. The widespread tendency to identify economic development with industrialization appears justified, since demographic pressures and over-all conditions limit the possibilities of development through the agricultural sector, and the trend in the terms of international trade for primary products has not been favorable to developing countries. Needless to say, this tendency is encouraged by the example of the advanced economies, in which, generally speaking, industry is the most important and dynamic sector of productive activity.

The Greek economy still has ample margin for a substantial rise in the efficiency and output of agriculture and animal husbandry, particularly if the crop structure is effectively readjusted. The importance attached to agricultural development in Greece is, therefore, justified. A substantial improvement in agricultural exports which form the backbone of Greek export trade, can and should be achieved.

In view, however, of the existing shortage of arable

---

[1] This chapter is a condensed version of the corresponding chapter of the Greek edition of this book.

land, the possibilities outlined above would not suffice to ensure a continuous increase in national product which would eventually enable the entire population of Greece to enjoy the income level prevailing in advanced economies. Indeed, agriculture is subject to the law of diminishing returns to a greater extent than any other sector of economic activity. In spite of the fact that technological developments often postpone the operative results of the "law," international experience has shown that the rates of increase in agricultural productivity and output are generally too low to accelerate a country's progress towards the level of a mature economy. Progress towards this goal is bound to be primarily the outcome of development in the industrial sector. The sector of services, on the other hand, although continually in process of expansion and of particular importance to the Greek economy as a significant source of foreign exchange (shipping, tourism, etc.), would not in itself suffice for a sustained acceleration of the country's over-all rate of economic progress. It should be noted that certain countries in which the service sector plays a prominent role, Switzerland for example, have taken steps to promote the simultaneous development of industry. Although the expansion of services is undoubtedly highly important to the Greek economy it would not be advisable to regard it as an adequate substitute for industrial development. Rapid industrialization, accompanied by balanced growth of the whole economy, is an imperative need in Greece for the following reasons:

First, as it is rather unlikely that Greek agricultural output will exhibit a spectacular and sustained rate of growth in the near future, the attainment of a relatively satisfactory average annual rate of growth in G.N.P. would require industrial output to increase at an appreciably higher rate. Industrial development is of crucial importance, if an increase is to be achieved in the absorptive capacity of the Greek economy and the limitations imposed by the balance

194

of payments on the maximization of the rate of economic development are to be alleviated. In other words, increased industrial output will enable an acceleration in the growth of national income without creating large external deficits as a result of higher imports.

Second, high rates of G.N.P. growth and increased per capita income are generally accompanied by a rapid rise in imports. It is important, though, to remember that in developing countries higher imports are not only the result of higher per capita income, which is usually combined with a strong propensity to import, but are also a condition for raising G.N.P., insofar as they consist of capital goods and raw materials indispensable to economic development. Most developing countries face acute difficulties in securing foreign exchange for the imports needed to accelerate their economic development. Thus, the weaknesses of the external sector of the economy are often the main factor which restricts the maximization of the rate of economic development.

In the Greek economy, the steadily improving development of invisible receipts has so far effectively offset the inadequacy of export earnings. It would be an error, however, to believe that in the years to come, the problem posed by the external sector of the Greek economy will be solved satisfactorily and safely in this way. Rapid industrial expansion is therefore needed, not only to satisfy a part of the rising import needs, but also to increase industrial exports. The most dynamic manufacturing units must be decisively oriented toward the export market. In the present favorable climate for greater liberalization of world trade, it is likely that the doubling of per capita income in Greece over the next decade will be accompanied by a corresponding increase in the volume of imports. It would be highly unrealistic to expect that these higher imports will be financed solely by an increase in agricultural exports and

195

current invisible earnings. Thus, the danger that the external sector of the Greek economy may become the major restrictive factor of economic development necessitates a rapid increase in industrial exports.

Third, most of the increase in the Greek labor force, excluding emigrants, has so far been absorbed by the sector of services. From the over-all point of view of the country's economic structure, this sector is already employing a number of people in excess of its real employment opportunities. Industrial expansion can play a major part in the rapid elimination of unemployment and underemployment and the reduction of emigration. As the efficient development of Greek industry depends on the achievement of international competitiveness, which in turn is connected with a substantial rise in productivity, it is obvious that there must be a particularly high rate of industrial expansion if the industrial sector is to make a decisive contribution towards raising employment levels. From this point of view, the industrialization effort should be considered as a foremost aim of social policy. It provides the best way to a permanent and satisfactory solution of employment problems.

Fourth, the industrialization of the Greek economy should be regarded as a basic condition for balanced regional development. Particular emphasis should be given to the development of industries which will exploit agricultural and mineral resources. The creation of industrial zones could be of vital importance to this end.

If the pronounced inequality in per capita income observed in the various regions of Greece continues, it may lead to the highly undesirable phenomenon of a "dual economy," if not to the depopulation of some areas and the overcrowding of urban centers. In conjunction with the development of the country's agricultural sector, a regionally balanced expansion of industrial activity is essential if this serious problem is to be tackled with success.

The Major Objectives of Greek Industrial Development

If the Greek industrialization effort is to succeed in accelerating the rate of economic expansion, improving the balance of payments, and raising employment levels, the most dynamic branches of industry must be oriented toward the export market. Industrial development can, and indeed should, be based in part on the substitution of imports. To some extent, this has already taken place. However, as stressed at the recent United Nations Trade and Development Conference in Geneva, the substitution of imports is not a sufficient outlet for rapid and wide-scale industrialization. International experience has shown that import substitution plays a relatively greater part in the initial stage of industrial expansion, whereas the possibilities for a substitution of imports are reduced sharply in more industrialized low-income countries, such as Greece. Apart from some basic disadvantages, which will be discussed below, plants that manufacture import substitutes are generally faced with the problem of rapidly rising production costs. They can contribute little towards economizing foreign exchange on account of their usually heavy dependence on imports of capital goods and intermediate products. It must be stressed, however, that the development of import-substituting industries in a wider economic region, such as the Common Market, is particularly important and offers great possibilities. But we must remember that these industries are in the export industry category of the country where they are established.

It is of special significance that the Trade and Development Conference gave general and unconditional emphasis to the need for expanding industrial exports—a need we have repeatedly underscored on many occasions. An example worth noting is that the rapid industrialization of centrally planned economies has necessarily been combined with a sharp expansion of their foreign trade, whereas these countries

197

were originally oriented towards a policy of self-sufficiency. Indeed, in the 1950's, the foreign trade of the centrally planned economies rose by an average annual rate of 12 per cent. This percentage is three times higher than the equivalent increase in the underdeveloped countries and about one-third above the figure for advanced economies in the rest of the world.

For a small and relatively low-income country such as Greece, the expansion of industrial exports is essential for the following main reasons:

1. The small size of the domestic market is a serious *obstacle to industrial development*. This applies both at industry and firm levels.

In many branches of modern industry the optimum size of manufacturing units, as determined by technological developments, exceeds the absorptive capacity of the domestic market. In these fields of industry, the establishment of industrial plants oriented exclusively towards the home market would oblige these enterprises to operate at sub-optimal production levels. The survival of such firms presumes the introduction of highly protective measures. These in their turn would facilitate the establishment of other inefficient industries, with adverse repercussions on the structure of the industrial sector, which would then consist of relatively small units operating at sub-optimal technological and economic levels. There are, of course, several branches of industry in which economies of scale are not important enough to preclude the profitable operation of smaller production units. This can be seen in the mature economies, where large industrial concerns operate side by side with small businesses. In the developing countries, however, regardless of differences in the size of the firm, the small, domestically oriented enterprises are substantially inferior to the larger export-oriented firms as regards business initiative, modernization, and rational organization. Consequently, the size

198

and orientation of industrial units in the developing countries directly influences their operating efficiency.

In a small and low-income country such as Greece, the domestic demand for each branch of manufacturing industry is usually insufficient and exhibits strong periodical fluctuations caused, after a certain time lag, by corresponding variations in agricultural output and income. Industry in the developing countries does not, as a rule, consist of closely interdependent complexes, and the agricultural sector is the main source of income and demand, with the inevitable consequence that industrial activity depends on largely uncontrollable fluctuations in agricultural production. This is proved by the Greek experience during the period under review. In these circumstances, instead of constituting the main expansionary force in economic development, the industrial sector is submitted to the influence of development in agriculture.

These obstacles and hindrances to industrial development can be eliminated to a considerable extent by orienting industry towards the export market.

2. Export orientation and the realization of exports by a given industrial concern are a strong incentive for rationalizing the organization and operation of the firm, and a safe criterion for evaluating its efficiency. If the firm is established with the purpose of exporting its products, it will also have to operate efficiently at internationally competitive levels. The realization of exports will be a reliable indicator of the success of this effort. In developing countries, industrial enterprises which aim at exporting their output to large and developed markets are technically, organizationally, and commercially far superior to those firms that are oriented mainly or exclusively towards the home market.

The advantages of export firms which we have just described, form a contrast to the sluggish rate of development generally found in import-substituting industries. With a protected market for their operations, the latter exhibit organizational and operational weaknesses and often expand into production lines of limited or even negative significance for economic development.

3. It would be hazardous for a small developing country, such as Greece, to ignore the strong trend toward liberalization of international trade and payments and to remain a mere spectator while wider economic regions are created. The effective development of the Greek economy within the present international environment depends essentially on the promotion of Greek industrial exports which now enjoy favorable prospects as a result of the country's association with the E.E.C.

It must be stressed that theoretical objections to a developing country's heavy dependence on foreign trade refer and apply to exports of primary products. On the contrary, the expansion of industrial exports on the basis of dynamic comparative advantages is imperative and is generally regarded as necessary for improving the external sector of developing countries and accelerating their rate of development. In the case of Greece, the realization of industrial exports on a wide and expanding scale presumes the removal of serious obstacles, in addition to the attainment of competitive cost levels. The fact that markets for industrial products are generally characterized by monopolistic competition makes it necessary to standardize Greek products at a satisfactory quality level, to differentiate them from others by trade marks, and to ensure prompt delivery in adequate quantities, etc.

The relative inexperience of businessmen in developing countries, the lack of organized trade networks capable of penetrating foreign markets, and the consequent increase in the element of risk are serious restrictive factors for the expansion of industrial exports. To eliminate these factors, export firms must be assisted by special organizations, (the Industrial Development Corporation in Greece, for example), while the advanced countries should give active encouragement to these activities.

It should be stressed, however, that one of the major obstacles in the way of industrial export expansion by low-income countries is the protectionist policy often applied by the industrial nations. In this connection, Greece has achieved favorable treatment through her association with the E.E.C.

THE INDUSTRIALIZATION OF GREECE AND THE ASSOCIATION WITH THE EUROPEAN ECONOMIC COMMUNITY

Greece's association with the E.E.C. provides the opportunity for development of export-oriented industrial production under advantageous conditions. Export orientation of industrial production has not become imperative merely as a result of the country's association with the Community; it is in any case indispensable for Greece and is decisively facilitated and encouraged by the Association Agreement. The advantages deriving from the association consist in the favorable treatment now enjoyed by Greek industrial products in the Common Market, where tariffs have already been reduced by 60 per cent and will be completely eliminated by the end of 1965 or 1966 at the latest.

It is sometimes argued, however, that these favorable conditions are of no value for Greece, as Greek industry cannot possibly take advantage of them. This argument can be refuted, both in a positive and a negative sense. On the negative side, it can be remarked that, accepting the argument as valid would, in essence, amount to denying the possibility of economic development, insofar as Greek economic progress presumes rapid industrial growth, which can mainly be achieved by exporting a considerable proportion of output. On the positive side, the argument can be refuted by the observation that, under the present prospects of a rapid income expansion in Europe, the production process is undergoing widespread readjustment from the point of view of international specialization, which will enable Greece to achieve considerable industrial development. Moreover, this development will consist not only of increasing the exports of existing or related industries, but in establishing new plants.

Greek product penetration into the E.E.C. is facilitated and encouraged by the following provisions in the Association Agreement between Greece and the Community:

1. While Greece will take advantage of E.E.C. tariff reductions with the added prospect that Community import duties will be completely eliminated by the end of 1965 or 1966, her home market will be almost entirely reserved for domestic industry for several years. Tariff reductions on imports of E.E.C. products also manufactured in Greece will total only 20 per cent in the first decade after the Association Agreement, i.e., up to the end of October 1972. Complete elimination of Greek import duties on E.E.C. products will not take place until 1984.

2. Pursuant to article 18 of the Association Agreement, Greece will have the right to introduce or raise the duties on imports of products manufactured for the first time in Greece up to 25 per cent *ad valorem*. This is a special provision in favor of new industries producing goods, the total import value of which did not exceed 10 per cent of Greece's imports from the Community in 1958. This ensures an ample margin, particularly if the protection given to newly established industries is specialized in the sense that it is extended for specific products, with an expected output considerably larger than domestic consumption. It should also be noted that up to the end of October 1974, Greece will be able to exercise this right unilaterally, merely by notifying the Association Council. The duties imposed or raised under article 18 may remain valid for a period of nine years, after which they will be gradually

202

reduced so as to be completely abolished by the end of the 22-years period, i.e., by the end of October 1984.

3. A basic principle of the Rome Treaty is that it prohibits subsidies and government aid within the E.E.C. barring exceptional cases under special procedures. However, according to article 52 of the Association Agreement, "....Greece shall be deemed to be in the situation referred to in paragraph 3 (a) of Article 92 of the Treaty establishing the Community.....," (i.e., it is grouped with regions "in which the standard of living is unusually low" or with regions "harassed by serious underemployment"). In this sense, the government assistance necessary to economic development can be granted.

MEASURES TO PROMOTE INDUSTRIALIZATION IN GREECE

The formulation of an effective policy to accelerate industrial development in Greece pre-supposes a systematic and detailed study of the economic, technological, and organizational aspects of the problem. An indicative enumeration of these aspects would include the determination and selection of those branches of industry which possess dynamic comparative advantages in accordance with the changing availability of the factors of production and developments in international demand; the improvement of technical equipment, production methods and productivity; the adjustment of the legislative and institutional framework to the needs of rapid industrialization; the establishment of enterprises of optimum size; the promotion of economic and technical research; the decentralization of industry and the sound financing of the industrial sector. An exhaustive investigation into these problems would lie beyond the scope of the present study. On broad lines, this study touches upon certain measures, the advisability of which is confirmed by the weaknesses and delays observed in Greek industry.

It is obvious that industrial development in Greece is directly related to the level and efficiency of investment in industry. As already stressed, industrial investment in recent years has been inadequate. As a result, the main policy aim should be to promote industrial investment at a rate commensurate with the ultimate objective of rapid industrial and economic expansion. An idea of the magnitude of this problem is given by estimates: an increase in national income by 6 or 7 per cent annually, requires gross industrial investment to rise from the 1963 level of 3,500 million drachmas, to between 7,000 and 9,000 million drachmas annually in the coming years.

Incentives can play an important role in mobilizing business initiative. It is widely recognized, however, that tax and duty discounts and exemptions, larger depreciation allowances, credit facilities, the simplification of controls, etc., have so far been of limited effect. This phenomenon, which is also observed in other countries, has given rise to the problem of readjusting the pattern of incentives, revising the extent of the advantages extended, and adapting policy measures to business psychology. The possibility of breaking through the grip of entrepreneurial inertia by increased benefits should be investigated. Moreover, it is also necessary to consider whether some incentives may lie beyond the limits of the businessman's economic horizon. If this is the case, the incentives will take effect in time through the gradual improvement of business standards and the broadening of the business outlook. But if such incentives are to have an immediate effect, it is imperative to complement them with measures adapted to current business psychology.

The limited effect of incentives is also largely attributable to the fact that they are neutralized by a series of counter-incentives. The elimination of counter-incentives is an indispensable condition to rapid and effective industrialization in Greece. They are largely related to the current system of government intervention which, as already stressed, consists of a multitude of uncoordinated and often contradictory measures which have accumulated over a long period of time and are now piled up in a chaotic whole. As a result, industrial activity is often discouraged without reason and is generally subject to the adverse effect of substantial obstacles and burdens which limit its efficiency and competitiveness. It is therefore of basic importance for the country's industrial development to reorganize the government departments and agencies involved and to simplify and rationalize government intervention techniques. The current system of licenses and controls for the industrial sector is so confused and creates such burdens and obstacles that any effort to improve it would be utterly futile. It should be replaced, as soon as possible, by a coherent, explicit, and coordinated system which will ensure the proper expansion of industrial activity. Structural changes in the industrial sector should also be combined with the restoration of competitive conditions in the home market.

The attraction of foreign capital for productive investment, especially in the form of mixed enterprises in collaboration with Greek firms, is highly important to the acceleration of industrial expansion. Large-scale inflow of foreign venture capital will substantially facilitate the rapid modernization and reorganization of Greek industry on the basis of the technical and organizational experience of the developed countries. It will also make a decisive contribution towards tackling the problem of foreign markets and the penetration of the trade networks of the advanced economies by Greek industrial concerns. Since the objective is to orientate the country's industrial development towards the export market to a greater degree than has hitherto been the case, when considering whether the inflow of foreign capital is advantageous to Greece, an essential criterion should be the level of investment undertaken in conjunction with a specified obligation to export part of the output. It is not advisable—though it has happened in the past—for firms

205

setting up in Greece to aim exclusively at the home market. Whenever collaboration between Greek and foreign capital is involved, the Greek economy will benefit most if a considerable portion of share capital remains in the hands of Greek entrepreneurs, or possibly of the Industrial Development Corporation, and if Greek personnel is appointed to responsible positions in the technical, organizational, and administrative spheres.

Greece's proximity to industrially and technically advanced countries of the West, combined with her monetary and foreign exchange stability and available labor force, are highly favorable factors for the attraction of foreign capital. Moreover, Greek economic and political relations with Middle Eastern and African countries are additional factors that can help to attract foreign private capital.

The availability of a sufficient labor force at low efficiency wages gains particular importance at a time when pressures in the European labor markets are strong. In the short run, the advanced countries of Western Europe are dealing with the problem of labor shortages through the admission of foreign workers. However, the high social costs entailed by the utilization of foreign labor, which has to be provided with housing, hospitals, etc., make it advantageous for these countries to favor the expansion of their enterprises into regions with a surplus labor force, such as Greece. The continuing economic progress of Western Europe is in any case gradually leading to the deconcentration of long-established industrial centers, where negative external economies are beginning to appear.

Foreign capital is already showing considerable interest in investing in Greece and in collaborating with Greek businessmen. To promote this, a series of contacts should be established with foreign firms to discover whether they are interested in setting up production units in Greece and to give them every encouragement. The establishment of Industrial Development Corporation agencies in large cities abroad would contribute considerably to this objective.

X

PROBLEMS AND PROSPECTS
OF THE AGRICULTURAL SECTOR[1]

THE ROLE OF THE AGRICULTURAL SECTOR IN THE DEVELOPMENT OF THE GREEK ECONOMY

The contribution of the agricultural sector to the growth process varies in quantity and quality according to the stage of development of the economy. In the initial stages, during which agriculture absorbs the highest percentage of the active population and has the largest share in the national product, the principal objective is to increase the production of basic foodstuffs to satisfy the expanding demand and raise the standard of food consumption. In this phase, incomes are very low and the main problem is to achieve a rate of increase in the agricultural supply commensurate with the rate of increase of demand. In later stages, when per capita income has increased, the agricultural sector has to cope with the problem of a low income elasticity of demand for traditional basic products, and faces the loss of labor force to other sectors which develop at a faster rate. Consequently, the development of the sector depends on the readjustment of crop structure according to the prospects of future demand—domestic and foreign—and on increased labor productivity which will compensate the gradual decrease in the number of people employed in the agricultural sector.

Greek agriculture has already advanced beyond the stages associated with an extensive cultivation of traditional crops. The continuous readjustment of production according

---

[1] This chapter is a condensed version of the corresponding chapter of the Greek edition of the book.

to trends in demand, as determined by the growth of income and the changes in consumers' tastes, has become a vital necessity for the further substantial development of the sector. Land and climatic conditions in Greece give a comparative advantage to a considerable number of agricultural products in the international market. This fact, in conjunction with the limited absorptive capacity of the domestic market, clearly suggests that all export opportunities ought to be fully exploited. Agricultural export products, which are now the largest single item in the country's exports, can and should be the dynamic propulsive factor of agricultural development. In addition to the expansion of exports of traditional products, such as tobacco, currants, etc., large export possibilities appear to exist for fruits and vegetables, cotton, and other products. To expand the list of agricultural exports, however, there should be a systematic research program and effective measures should be taken in the following directions:

First, the crop structure must be readjusted after a thorough study of all potential alternative products, followed by a new and rational selection. In the past, efforts to achieve a readjustment of crop structure have been limited to a small number of new products, notably cotton, and it is probable that there are a variety of other products which are equally well, if not better, suited to be profitably substituted for the extensive cultivation of traditional crops.

Second, systematic marketing research must be carried on. An indispensable prerequisite for the success of the whole program is the methodical and detailed study of existing and prospective conditions in the domestic and— even more important—in the foreign market. Since most Greek export products enter the world market under conditions of monopolistic competition, the quality, packaging, quantity on offer and time of delivery, standardization etc., are important factors which should be studied carefully.

Furthermore, inasmuch as agricultural production is export oriented, an improvement in productivity and the reduction of production costs to international levels are imperative.

On general lines, an effective agricultural policy should include a series of coordinated and mutually complementary measures towards an efficient utilization of available land, a high rate of development investment, and an improvement of the human factor. There are, of course, a number of other factors that need improvement in order to attain a high rate of agricultural development, such as agricultural credit, the organization of farmers' cooperatives, technical research and experimentation, etc.

EFFICIENT LAND UTILIZATION

The success of a program of public investment in the agricultural sector depends fundamentally on the existence of viable agricultural production units. The real objective in this case is the transformation of agricultural establishments from family subsistence nuclei into viable farming enterprises. Under existing conditions in Greece, the achievement of this aim depends on widespread land consolidation increasing the size of farms.

Land consolidation

The problem of land reform in Greece appears acute and there has been only limited progress towards solving it during the postwar period. Land fragmentation creates many obstacles in all stages of the production process. It hinders the systematic organization of agricultural production and the application of intensive cultivation methods. In general, the use of modern agricultural machinery becomes very difficult or even impossible. The irrigation of highly fragmented agricultural properties is complicated and costly. Land fragmentation also entails the loss

of arable land, which is wasted in the extensive network of
roads, paths, and boundaries connecting or separating the
numerous sections. Lastly, the long distances between
several land plots of common ownership consume both time
and effort during both cultivation and harvest periods.
According to some studies, land consolidation alone would
increase the income of the farmers concerned by some 100
to 200 per cent. Hence, land reform appears to be one of
the most important factors in raising agricultural income.

According to a sample survey conducted by the Ministry
of Agriculture, covering 1,428 farms in all regions, land
fragmentation in Greece is acute (see Table 60).

TABLE 60

Land fragmentation in Greece

Areas	Average size of farm (hectares)	Average number of land plots by farm	Average size of land plots (hectares)	Average dispersion of farm plots (Klms)
Macedonia	4.53	7.5	0.61	2.5
Thessaly	6.81	10.0	0.68	2.4
Central Greece	8.57	11.0	0.78	2.8
Peloponnesus	5.68	7.9	0.72	2.2
Islands	5.99	12.5	0.48	2.2
Total area	5.99	9.2	0.65	2.5

Source: Ministry of Agriculture.

Table 60 shows that the average number of land plots
constituting one farm was nowhere less than 7, while the
average dispersion was 2.5 kilometers.

The results of efforts to effect land consolidation have
so far been rather poor. From 1953, when the existing
legislation for land consolidation was enacted, until the end
of 1962, land reform has proceeded at the rate shown in
Table 61.

210

Up to 1958, land consolidation took place on a voluntary basis at the request of the majority of farmers involved. From 1959 onwards compulsory consolidation was introduced in

TABLE 61

Progress in land reform during the postwar period

Year	Villages	Area (in thousands of hectares)	Number of farm plots (thousands)		Number of farmers (thousands)
			Before land reform	After land reform	
1953	4	2.01	16.9	0.7	0.4
1954	6	3.81	25.2	2.1	1.0
1955	6	3.44	62.4	3.4	1.5
1956	10	8.06	38.3	3.1	2.2
1957	6	4.16	9.8	1.4	0.8
1958	6	6.65	38.7	4.5	2.3
1959	9	6.58	28.3	3.5	2.0
1960	33	19.73	54.4	9.2	5.8
1961	24	21.02	42.1	6.4	4.9
1962	60	32.00	92.5	17.5	8.7
Total	164	107.46	418.4	51.9	38.4

Source: Ministry of Agriculture.

certain cases. According to expert estimates, 1.2 million hectares should be subject to land reform in the next decade. It appears, however, that if this faster rate of land consolidation is to be achieved, the compulsory consolidation of land plots will have to be extended.

Enlargement of agricultural establishments

The consolidation of farm properties will not suffice to solve the problem of small farms. In the course of the last twenty years, the number of small farms has been steadily decreasing in all European countries. This development is related to

211

the inability of small farms to use new technical methods and to compete effectively against large farms. No data are as yet available in Greece on the reduction in the number of small farms. The present number of small farm establishments in Greece is estimated to be 25 per cent of the total.

TABLE 62

Size of farm establishments in Greece

Area in hectares	Number of farms (in thousands)	Per cent
0 — 0.1	10.0	1.0
0.1 — 1	276.7	27.5
1 — 5	573.2	56.9
5 — 10	114.3	11.4
10 — 20	25.9	2.6
20 — 50	5.4	0.5
50 and over	1.0	0.1
	1,006.6	100.0

Source: Agriculture Census, 1950.

Since the enlargement of farm property into viable agricultural establishments is a necessity, strong incentives should be created, including low interest or noninterest bearing loans for the purchase of land and the subsidization of purchases of agricultural equipment. One condition should be imposed, namely that the beneficiaries will enlarge their land property by an appropriate number of hectares. Furthermore, legislative measures should be enacted to determine the conditions that farms should fulfill. A special case would be the determination of the conditions under which a farm would be subject to compulsory sale if the owner had abandoned its cultivation. Legislative provisions should also prevent a further fragmentation of land property through hereditary succession.

The optimum size of farm establishment

In order to bring about proper land consolidation and farm enlargement, it is necessary to carry out a research project on factors and considerations which should determine the optimum size of a farming unit. From the technico-economic point of view, the type of products under cultivation and the methods of marketing determine an optimum combination of capital equipment, size of land, and technical capacity of labor. From the sociopolitical view a farm unit can be considered optimum if it secures a satisfactory income to the farmer's family (roughly corresponding to the income which could be earned by the farmer in other sectors). Obviously, from both viewpoints, the factors determining the optimum farm size are apt to change with time, especially in a growing economy. Consequently, the optimum farm size as a standard unit, will have to be readjusted in accordance with developments in technology and the trend of income levels. Moreover, inasmuch as the income of the urban sector tends to increase, the enlargement of farming units will be necessary if the rural economy is to retain the labor capacity it requires. This consideration points to the need of supplying a more extensive social infrastructure in order to provide better education, improved health conditions, more and better opportunities for recreation, entertainment etc. It should be noted that the income disparities between the urban and rural sectors in favor of the former are not, as a rule, sufficient to cause an efficient reallocation of population between sectors, corresponding to the needs of economic development. As a result, a substantially lower rate of increase is observed in agricultural per capita income and entails a complex and costly system of government income support policies. Such problems could be avoided if the proper studies were made and measures were taken to establish an effective mechanism for the readjustment of farming units to the optimum size.

The objective of development policy for the agricultural sector in Greece should be a sufficient enlargement in the size of farms to achieve a satisfactory increase in agricultural income and eliminate the need for inefficient subsidization policies. According to some estimates, over half of the farms in Greece today are not economically viable. This is one of the more serious obstacles to the development of Greek agriculture; these small units are unable to contribute significantly to the development process and, in several instances, they have not proved able to avail themselves of the new opportunities opened by the program of public investment in agriculture.

INVESTMENT EXPENDITURE

Land improvements

The increase of production per land unit—through better crop selection or an increase in the yields of existing cultivations—is closely related to the construction of basic land improvement works, especially in the field of irrigation. The extension of irrigation is considered to be the most important factor for raising agricultural productivity in Greece. Today, only 12 per cent of total cultivated land is irrigated, but intensive efforts are being made to extend irrigation.

Another important problem is the speedy utilization of improved land areas. It calls for a considerable number of parallel small private investment projects, a higher level of technical efficiency and a properly working system of marketing new products. In fact, it has been estimated that the full readjustment of agricultural production to new land conditions takes from five to ten years from the time when the secondary investment works are completed. This lag can be substantially shortened by an early and intensive information program directed toward farmers on the technical and economic subjects related to new production conditions, and /or by the government undertaking a part of the supplementary networks.

214

Machinery and equipment

The expansion of the mechanization of agricultural production is a basic factor in raising productivity. It also provides a buffer capacity during periods of peak employment and significantly assists the promotion of animal husbandry. Mechanization also helps the timely cultivation of land and reduces the dangers of crop losses through adverse weather conditions. The introduction of new production methods is also greatly facilitated and there is a substantial reduction in the need for human labor as a result of mechanization. According to experts, the use of mechanical means of production releases 25 to 70 per cent of the labor previously employed.

Agricultural mechanization in Greece has expanded at a fast pace during the last fifteen years. The number of machines in use increased by 300 per cent. This high rate is due to significant improvements in the technical field during the postwar period which enabled the multiple use of tractors, an increase in agricultural income, better credit facilities, and the great improvement in productivity per hectare caused by mechanization. There are several indications that wide margins exist for an extension of mechanization in Greek agriculture. It should be noted, however, that although an increased number of workers have been released by the introduction of mechanical means of production, they have not been productively absorbed by other sectors. Under such conditions, the increase in productivity loses a large portion of its social and economic significance. The mechanization of agriculture, therefore, should be kept in balance with the development of the absorptive capacity of the labor market in other sectors.

THE HUMAN FACTOR AND THE DEVELOPMENT OF GREEK AGRICULTURE

An increase in investment expenditure, faster progress in land consolidation, and the enlargement of farming units

215

form the essential framework for the development of Greek agriculture. Any program of public investment, however, will have difficulty in reaching its targets unless the human factor is properly adjusted to it. This adjustment is directly related to the level of technical education in the farm population. Inadequate technical training will manifest itself in inability to apply new methods of cultivation and in lack of entrepreneurial spirit and flexibility in adjusting production to market conditions. This problem of the human factor is especially serious in agricultural production, because the number of persons requiring technical knowledge and initiative is very large. Hence an effective educational program must be organized to cover a large part of the agricultural population.

The educational level of the Greek agricultural population is clearly higher than that in other less-developed countries, where the use of modern technical methods is inhibited not only by lack of knowledge but by racial, social, or religious obstacles. Yet, a considerable section of the agricultural population, especially farmers who live in mountainous areas, lacks sufficient knowledge of modern methods of production. The adverse effects of the low level of education are especially evident in the delay observed in the utilization of irrigation works and the reluctance shown in undertaking secondary parallel investments.

These inadequacies in the agricultural population are mainly due to defects in the educational system. Elementary education, common to all areas and professions, was not adjusted to the special conditions and needs of the agricultural population. Instructions for improving cultivation methods are given by agronomists trained in the few agricultural colleges, too few to cover all but a small part of the country. Hence, qualified persons are not available who combine theoretical knowledge with practical experience and who can be in continuous contact with the farmers. Despite the variety of agricultural schools existing in Greece, the

216

training they offer is generally rather inadequate. Thus, to achieve the required improvement in the technical education of the agricultural labor force, a reformation and expansion of the existing educational system is necessary.

Efforts should be directed mainly towards educating the younger generation. The ability of the adult population to absorb new technical knowledge and to familiarize itself with new means and methods is rather limited, due to the innate conservatism of farmers and their adherence to tradition. The appropriate preparation for learning new technical methods should be started when the student is very young.

A Revision of Income Support Policies and the Readjustment of Crop Structure

The agricultural price support policies pursued thus far in Greece have on the whole conflicted with the objectives of the over-all agricultural policy which was aimed at effecting the desired readjustment of crop structure.

Since it is not feasible to abandon agricultural income support policies, for sociopolitical and other reasons, the problem is to devise methods of protection that will at the same time work as incentives for structural improvements in production. For this purpose protective policies should be specifically pursued with regard both to products and areas. Since local productive conditions differ from area to area, incentives for crop structure readjustment granted in the form of protective policies would be effective only if they were suitably adjusted to the particular area and products. In other cases where protective policies are primarily followed to raise agricultural yields, rather than bring about readjustment in the crop structure, support should take the form of subsidizing the price of the means of production, or of more intense governmental efforts for improving the organization of agricultural production. Finally,

217

in cases where the technical possibilities of crop readjustment are lacking and the income-raising objective is urgent, it would be preferable to adopt direct income payments to farmers rather than to fix support prices for a crop. These payments could be tied to some obligation for farmers to improve their means or methods of production, and should be independent of the kind of product under cultivation.

These changes would assist and accelerate the reorientation of Greek agriculture in conformity with present and prospective trends in world demand without reducing the existing support of agricultural income.

INDEX

219

GPSR Authorized Representative: Easy Access System Europe - Mustamäe tee
50, 10621 Tallinn, Estonia, gpsr.requests@easproject.com

www.ingramcontent.com/pod-product-compliance
Lightning Source LLC
Chambersburg PA
CBHW061159220326
41599CB00025B/4533